tures, full
s remote.
3-1181

852

'cart. 20EN
or 578-4887

ereo, Mar-
oneer turn-
best offer,
y Ward 8
der deck &
er 6:30pm

SYSTEM
me brand.

iver, BSR
r speakers,
OBO, 782-

watt receiv-
Mitsubishi
). 492-0755

mp, amp,
eck, Janzen
796-8559

707 reel to
cass, GSL
ll! 492-2622

ate compo-

Deck—8-
90 minute
913

eiver 125
echnics dir
83-6519

and JBL
ents. Any-
621-6484

S 854

iano, excel
will move,

Bramback,
341-2514

, full con-
e combina-
must sell,

d.
vory, beau-
ction. $450.
etween 12-4,
56-3988

ante 2 Yrs.
ut, 4 Yrs.
2

ND-PIANO
-4966

2 yrs old,
8-3934

new, 75 yr
und board.

with Swin-
automatic
Very good
best offer.
ob

honic Holi-
d 229-6673

Magic Gen-
50. 453-6369

boree—per-
, fully
532-4531

dual kybd
841-1280

B DRUM
d & stand.
31-3154

Grand pia-
pico mech-
nish, mint
42 or 383-

piano, 2
cond, $2000
Lawrence

AND 1920-
nd. Serious
22

nd Piano,
-5793

RK CON-

---

... Collegiate, $150 or best offer 913-236-5923

TRUMPET—Holton with case, like new, Call Terri after 5:30pm 523-1821

TRUMPET-Professional Silver Olds Super Star, excellent condition, $225. 454-9090

TRUMPET-TROMBONE Brand new Bundys-cheap 621-6276

TRUMPETS—(2), after 6pm or weekends call 453-6388

VIOLIN-19th Century French, handsome, good tone, bow, case $700. 362-3357 evenings

VIOLIN—Full size, 2 years old, like new, $125, evenings only, 268-4110

VIOLIN ¾ size, Lewis, case & bow, excellent 356-9675

VIOLIN-Student, new, $285. 356-0201

YAMAHA—CP-70B elec, grand, excl. 942-5208

YAMAHA—MT-44, 4-track cass. recorder, $700 Mike 913-843-7559 Lawrence

PEDAL STEEL GUITAR Emmons D10. 383-3221

## MUSICAL INSTRUMENT AMPLIFICATION EQUIP. 859

AMPEG V4B Bass amp, spkrs, Peavey 2-15 cab w/ev's, Peavey 2-15 bin, Peavey 12PA mids w/ev's, mikes, timbales. 531-8610

PEAVY DUECE—XR600 w/2-112110TS SP, 260 monitor amp, 2-12, 2-15 cabinets, Music Man 2-12, Dean Markley RM80DR-112SC 942-3584

DC-Crown Pwr amp. $350. 796-6804

FENDER—Band Master. 50 wt 2 pyle 12" $150 587-8810

FENDER Bassman Amp—W/twin altec speakers. Excel all purpose amp. Jim, 722-3285

FENDER TWIN REVERB—2-12 $225. 913-682-4831

MARSHALL 1/2 Stack, lt. syst., sm. mixing board, power amp, monitor, must sell. 587-9756

MARSHALL-Cabinet 4-12's, $325. 913-682-4831

MXR—Digitial time delay. $300. Also, Conn strobotuner $250 761-4775

PA—Bass cabinets, 300 RMS, 2-15's ea. $250 for pair. 741-1080

SAXOPHONE—Alto, Leblanc, Vito, w-case, good cond, $225, 524-2353

WURLITZER-elec. piano $400, Sunn Amp. w-speaker cab. $400, or best offer, 753-8167

## CAMERA EQUIPMENT & SUPPLIES 861

KODAK-New sound Super 8 w/projector $325. 358-4511

LEICA IIIf, 35,50,85 lenses, more. $325. 913-843-5110

MAMIYA 645J W PD prism, 110mm, 210mm lenses + grip. $500 Pentax ME super body & motor drive $110. Pentax K1000 & F2.0 50mm lens $90. Yashica mat TLR $30. 492-6105 after 6pm

MINOLTA—35mm w/lenses. Best offer. 923-6004

MINOLTA XG1 2880 zoom, 50mm 135 mm, flash, gadget bag $350. 796-8559

MINOLTA XG7 35mm, all attachments including new 80x200mm zoom lens, camera bag, instruction books, etc. $350 for all. 483-0194

NIKONOS IV A-Used once, perfect. 816-232-8001 eves

---

... David 913-272-7511

IBM/PC 256K display printer, mint condition. $2400. 913-286-2740

MCINTOSH—with printer, software and carrying case 764-8928

MONITOR—new Amdek color II, IBM & Apple compatible, call aft 5 Pm or on weekends, 268-9047

PRINTER Centronics 101, stand, $150, 531-4869

SANYO 550 computer system, 128K, exp. to 256K, printer, monitor, software, under warranty. 453-2102

TRS-80 Model III, 1 disk drive, cass, modem, sound synthesizer, basic software $750 or best offer 358-3129

TRS 80 PC II with printer, $200 OBO, 764-4745, 782-0559

VICTOR 9000-10MB, 256K + software. Almost unused cond $4500. 631-5389

ZENITH—Z-100 Desk top Computer. 192K, two 360K disk dr, built-in monitor, lots of software, 4 mo old. $2,475. 816-531-0380

1ST STOP SOFTWARE NOW HAS FLIGHT SIMULATOR II from Sublogic FOR ATARI IN STOCK, 1 blk W 36th Noland, Indep, 816-254-4070

## OFFICE FURNITURE 875

DESK—Exec, walnut over steel construction, 722-3020

DESKS, CHAIRS, FILES—Conference, Safes, credenzas, bookcases, New-Used. 250 items. Save 50% Kelley's, 7740 Troost, 523-0447

DESKS-metal, wooden, secty chair, $75, 299-9291

OFFICE SALE-Beautiful desk & Credenza; Baker table; Oil paintings; Easy Chairs; Office chairs and more. Sale takes place: 10'O clock am to 6pm, Sept, 13, 14, 15 at: Argyle Bldg, 306 E 12th St. KC Missouri, suite 643, Terms, cash only

## OFFICE MACHINES & EQUIPMENT 877

ADLER Model 1005, fully electronic print wheel typewriter w/dual pitch. 888-4420

COPIER—Royal, paid $4500, sacrifice $1800. Still smells new. 931-6837

IBM correcting Selectric II typewriter, word processing system, Pitney Bowes postage machine, letter & legal hanging file folders. 453-2102

IBM—Display writer word processor, 5218 Printer, 60 CPS, sheet feed, paper handler, communications, qualifies for IBM maintenance. David, 913-272-7511

TYPEWRITER—Silver Reed, 6 K memory, 1 yr old, paid $600, sacrifice $250, 781-5453

## COMMERCIAL EQUIPMENT 880

BASEMENT forming system, alum. forms, 220+ tall, 500+ short, 417-876-2866, no collect

PRINTING EQUIPMENT

Due to companies merging we have the following for sale: Harris Aurelia 19x26, Chief w/T-51, Ludlow & accessories, proof press, slug surfacer, Brown 4000 camera, 350 A. B. Dick, 3M plate camera, multi WL 11x17, 10x15 Kluge, type &

---

16 WIDE—New, selling at factory invoice, park space available, take trade 287-1024, 642-8143

MOVE RIGHT IN 12x65 2 br front dining, all appliances, wetbar, shed, deck, skirted, 1 owner, exc cond 461-3822

SKYLINE—1973 12'x60' 2 bdrm, stove, refrig. new drapes, c/a, storage shed, $6,000 Indep. area 353-1350

Must sell. 1978 14x70 Hillcrest. c-a, energy efficient, lots of xtras, wood shed, excl cnd 795-0611 524-4636

CAMERON 1975, 14x70, 2 br, ac, W/D, stove & refrig, deck & shed, Lakeview Mobile Park. 454-6524 after 4

14X60 METAMORA-2 br, crpt, a/c, w/d, refrig, stove, deck, awning, shed, skirting, Lakeview Terrace 453-6361

DOUBLE WIDE—c/a, all crptd, wbfp, River Oaks Park. Owner 788-3601

DOUBLE wide, nice 3 bedroom, furnished, fenced yard, quiet, shady lot, cable TV, 924-6876

14X64—2 BDRM, Super clean & much new in & out, wood deck, come and look 829-8354, 1-913-883-2970

FAIRMONT—1982, 3 bdrm 2 ba front kitchen, garden tub, wood siding, negot. $1,800 assumes. 792-1450.

NICE—1966 12x60, awning, Morgan shed, wooden deck, complete furnishings. 923-0574 eves, & before 8am

REAL NICE—1 br trailer, newly remodeled, perf. for single person, newlyweds. or lake, 921-3941

WINSTON—1976 12 x 60 , 2 bdrm, appliances, ca, steel skirting, best offer, must sell. 816-732-4384

BROADMOOR-24x60 3br-2ba appl's, air, fenced, poss. fin avail 421-7720 816-352-6281

2 bed, fireplace, air, patio cover extras, must sell. $235 Mo. incls Lot Rent, 923-4485

1969 SKYLINE 3 br, 1 1/2 ba, 12 x 60. $6000 or offer. 816-229-5760 or 765-3082

I BUY MOBILE HOMES
CASH IN 24HRS 923-4000

10X55—Furnished. New carpet, a-c, lg porch. Asking $3,500, neg. 816-732-6687

WINSTON—1981, 14x65, like new, $12,000, wkdys 913-294-2415, wknd 816-252-8643.

SKYLINE-1978, 14x70 unfurn, $10,000. Must sell 454-5384, 587-8097

1980 MARSHFIELD-14x70 3 Br, 2 ba, c-a, will relocate. 649-8433 or 765-5242

WINSTON—1976, 14x70, 2 bedroom, 2 bath, Northgate Mobile Park, 436-0753

1977 Monte Carlo, 2 bdrm, all electric, many extras, owner will finance. 331-1182

CLOSING OUT SALE
Good Buys On Used 10'-12' Wides, 6900 E. 40 Hwy

1978 Mobile home, 12X60 2 bdrm, good shape, all electric, $5500. Call 913-287-4804

WINSTON—1982, 14x70, excel cond, see to appreciate, furn and all appls, 642-3063

CONCORD—1975 14X60 2br, set up for wood stove, reasonable. Tonganoxie 845-2926

CHAMPION-1972, 3 br, 13/4 ba, a/c, good cond 461-7705

COUNTRYSIDE-1980 14x60, 2 br assume loan 631-3438

12X60—1970 LTD $2750. Aft 7PM 464-5850

RENTAL Purchase Plan Mobile Home $215 923-4000

NICE PARK-NORTH-14x70

---

221-4555
722 WALNU
equal housing opp
Professionally Ma
Robert Esrey &

★ ★ ★ ★ ★ ★ ★

910 PE

HEAT A-C WATE
★CARPET, DRAP
★SECURE BUILD
★GREAT VIEWS
★SWIMMING POO
★GARAGE/RES. P
★1 BDRM FROM $
★2 BDRM FROM $

471-731

★ ★ ★ ★ ★ ★ ★

## UNFURN. APTS.— N.E. KCMO

CLEAN—1br apt. bus line close, 483-5

SEPTEMBER SP
Deluxe 1 bedroo
move in price $235.
2 br kids pets $185.
RENT GUIDE $

## UNFURN. APTS.— S. OF 27TH

30TH, 926 E—1 bd
Studio $160. All util
ture adults. Sec $
refs. 931-5542, 753-19

33rd-3br $190! 432-7
RENT GUIDE $

★★★★★★★★★
38TH & WARWICK
ba, deluxe, lndry
prkng, $340-$370

STUDIO-All utils pd
No pets.
931-1022
★★★★★★★★★

40TH—1-2 BR appl
adults $179. 753-1314

BALTIMORE—3632
garden apt, $325,
dren, no dogs, 56
appointment

BROADWAY-Valen
cious 2 bdrm, park
dry, hardwood flrs
adults only, dep. re
$295, 753-6449, 831-09

BROADWAY & V
adults only, except
ue, 2 bedroom, 931-

CROWN CENTER-
low area, luxurious
$200 mo, 221-5136

HYDE PARK—402
son, 2 BR, a-c, gas
carpet, cable TV,
parking, laundry,
paid. $275. 561-4029

KU MED
1 & 2 Bdrm Du
Apts. a/c, crpt, off
laund. fac. $235-$32

KU MED
Just reduced 4201
br air crpt drapes
appls prk Clean &
$255. 262-7950, 362-07

MEYER Blvd &
Park, Nice 1-2-
twnhse dplx $255 up

MEYER-Near Che
cious 3 bdrm, 2 ba
forml din rm, br
screen porch, c/a,
garage, $500 mo 56

MIDTOWN STU
Laundry & Conv.
bldg. Short term le
CLYDE MANOR

# SECULAR
# SANCTITY

To Tom Turkle
whose loyalty,
sacrifice and labor
helped a dream
to be born.

# SECULAR SANCTITY

Written

and

Illustrated

by

# Edward Hays

Forest of Peace Books, Inc.
Easton, KS 66020

# SECULAR SANCTITY

Library of Congress Catalog Card Number: 84-81954
ISBN 0-939516-05-5

*published by*
Forest of Peace Books, Inc.
Route One—Box 247
Easton, Kansas 66020

*printed by*
Hall Directory, Inc.
Topeka, Kansas 66608

Revised Edition: November 1984

Grateful acknowledgement for the use of material in the original photograph collages of this book is given to the following:
Michelangelo: *God Separating Water from the Earth, The Last Judgement, The Creation of Adam,* Sistine Chapel, Rome, Italy. Duccio di Boninsegna: *Christ Appears behind Closed Doors, Madonna in Her Majesty,* Siena, Italy (Alinari). Masaccio: *The Expulsion from Paradise,* Brancacci Church, Florence, Italy. Fra Angelico: *The Annunciation,* Museo del Gesu, Cortona, Italy, *Christ Scorned,* Convent of San Marco, Florence, Italy (Alinari). *St. Gregory and Scribes,* Kunshistorisches Museum, Vienna, Austria. Albrecht Durer: *Life of the Virgin, Angel of the Apocalypse, St. Jerome, Last Supper.* Brugel: *Summer.* A Turkish Artist: *Sultan Mohammed II.* Giotto: *Scrovegni Dedicating His Chapel,* Arena Chapel, Padua, Italy. Diego Valasquez: *The Coronation of the Virgin,* Prado Gallery, Madrid, Spain (Anderson). Bartel Bruyn: *The Annunciation.* Pietro Lorenzetti: *Madonna and Child,* Assisi, Italy (Alinari). Russian Ikons, Icon Deesis Festival Tier, Novogorod School, Our Savior, Moscow, USSR. Small Ikons, Euchology, Moscow, USSR. Basili Ivanovich Khokhlov: *Saint John on Pathmos,* Palekh, USSR. Vasili Skopin: *Silent is All Flesh. Ikonen-Kunststube Friefrau von Mauchenheim: Ikon of January and March,* Frankfurt, Germany. Andrei Rublev: *The Trinity,* Tretyakov Gallery, Moscow, USSR – UNESCO World Art Series. George Filippakis: *Icon of St. Photios the Great,* St. Photios National Greek Orthodox Shrine, St. Augustine, Florida. St. George Ikon, Lenningrad, USSR. *The Prophet Elijah,* Tretyakov Gallery, Moscow, USSR – UNESCO World Art Series. Ikon of Christ's Baptism, Russian. Marc Klionsky: *Night Thoughts.* William Bailey: *Still Life – Monterchi.* Anne Norcia: *Globular Cluster of Stars.* Jackson Pollock: *Autumn Rhythm.* Katsukawa Shunsho: *Snow, Moonlight and Flowers. Siva and Parvati,* Kangra Painting. *The Judgement of Paris, Pan and a Bacchanate,* National Museum, Naples, Italy. *Han Hsiang-Tzu, "Patron Saint" of Musicians,* Seligman Collection, *New Larousse Encyclopedia of Mythology. Rabbi with Tallit, Jewish Catalog. Pushkin, Connoisseur Magazine.* Dover Pictorial Archives Series. Theodore Roosevelt: *Letter to His Son, American Heritage.* Groote Kerke: *Organ,* Harrlem, Holland. Eliot Elisofon: *Arunachaleshvara Temple.* Lauros-Giraudon: *Chartres Cathedral. Zeus Meilichios,* Piraeus, Greece. Atomic Explosion, U.S. Defense Dept. Earth from the Moon, NASA. Photographers: Peter Lacy, Fairchild Aerial Surveys, Inc., Port of New York Authority; Henry Rapisardo, Level House; Fritz Henle, Parker-Brand Corp., Novosti; Margaret Bourke-White; Alfred Eisenstaedt, Bay Area Transit; Lee Blodgett; Glenn Christiansen; Robert Cox; Gerald Fredrick; Peter Fronk; Bob Hollingsworth; Ells Marugg; Mike McCurry; Jack McDowell; Norman Plate; Bill Plummer; Richard Rowan; Norman Prince; Tom Tracy; Peter O'Whiteley; Nikolya Zurek; McLeod Voltz; and Andre Keretsz. The Greater Kansas City Telephone Book, Southwestern Bell. And *The Kansas City Star and Times,* Kansas City, Missouri.

# Acknowledgements

The author wishes to express special gratitude to the many people who were responsible for the publication of this book, particularly:

Thomas Turkle, managing editor
Thomas Skorupa, editing and layout
Ruth Slickman, editing

David DeRusseau, art consultant

Mary Rau, who in her encouragement and energy was the catalyst for the first edition of this book.


I would like to thank the following for their creative work in the technical production of this book:

Custom Color Corporation of Kansas City, Missouri for the exacting reproduction of the black and white photographic art. Special thanks to Kevin Anderson and Rick Chasteen for their craftsmanship, and to Diana Star Kaye, Harold Teevan and Joel Seidelman for their patience and courteous service.

Gazlay Graphics, Inc. of Kansas City, Missouri for the precision work on the color separation for the cover, and especially Jan Seidelman for her kind assistance.

Mainline Printing, Inc. of Topeka, Kansas for the quality printing of the cover.

Steve and Cliff Hall of Hall Directory, Inc. of Topeka, Kansas and all their wonderful staff for their care and fine workmanship in the execution of the numerous details involved in the printing of this book.

# Contents

A Revised Edition?................10

Love the World with All Your Heart....13

Organic Reading: Teacher and Guide....19

Work: Blessing or Curse?............29

Love Your Money...................37

Home-Church-Shrine................45

The Primal Sacrament...............53

Prayer and the Bathroom...........63

A Sexual Spirituality...............73

Basic Disarmament and World Peace....83

21st Century Prophets.............93

The Web-Communion of Saints.......105

¿The Virtue of Questioning?.........115

The Mother of All Prayer: Gratitude...123

The Sacred Art of Letter Writing......131

The Necessity of Idleness...........141

Music: Gift from the Gods..........151

The Love of Death and Life.........159

Conclusion: The Best-Kept Secret......166

Author's Page...................173

# A Revised Edition ?

The twentieth century has radically changed the way we look at God, ourselves and the world. So fundamental has been the change that this time in history could well be viewed as a new era. We could speak appropriately of the year 1985 as "40 A.H." (After Hiroshima) or "A.A." (After Auschwitz). These and other events in the second half of this century have profoundly altered the way we look at life and ourselves. They have been like a giant tidal wave that has engulfed many of the secure foundations upon which we have built our lives and our relationships with God and one another. Education, marriage, industry, the arts and religion have all been swept up in the nuclear force of great change.

Those who emerged from the onslaught of the past forty years were left, like Noah and his family, with only the clothing on their backs and a few keepsakes. Gone, for the serious spiritual seeker, were the ageless symbols that had been regarded as sacred; gone were sacred times, sacred spaces and sacred persons. Swept away in the social tidal wave were the once clear distinctions between the sacred and the secular — so that now society appears to be wholly secular.

Some of the survivors attempted to "return" to the Bible, to the fundamental traditions and understanding of the past. But this attempt was futile. The environment of the old ways had vanished, and that time in history when the sacred was recognized by commonly embraced symbols had been swept away.

An awesome new task faced the spiritual person: the challenge to create a new spirituality for a new age. While some looked to the past, still others looked to the religions of the Orient for ways to find peace and depth of feeling. But searching the past or exploring

other religious cultures usually failed to provide the nourishment of spirit necessary for those living in the West at the end of the twentieth century. This is a unique historical period; no other age in history has been so devoid of the divine, so seemingly absent of the presence of God.

What is needed is a new way of seeing. We need to form a new vision of the sacred as the vibrant dimension hidden within the secular. We must find a way to end the separation — a way to join the two in a wedding, a fusion. Seeing the holy within the profane does not mean that we abandon prayer, worship and reverence for the sacred; it means rather that we look for the sacred in those things that we call "commonplace." This will not be an easy task, since we have no tradition which allows us to experience all of life as a central part of the Divine Mystery.

This edition of *Secular Sanctity* is a revision of an earlier text. We all know that we live in a world of rapid change. When a book is published it has already been a couple of years since it flowed from the heart and pen of the author. It must pass through the refinery of corrections by editors, the long process of typesetting and printing and, finally, of distribution to bookstores. By the time any book is finally in the hands of the reader, the author usually longs to rewrite and update its contents. This second edition, which originally appeared several years ago, gives this author that rare privilege.

With the book comes my wish that it will be the beginning of a growth process for you, the reader, to form a new and dynamic spirituality. May the new chapters and the revised text of the original chapters that follow in this book open an inner vision for you — a vision in which you will begin to see the ordinary, everyday events of your life become electric with divine energy.

11

# Love the World
# with All Your Heart

If you were looking for a guru, you wouldn't choose your local grocer. Few plumbers are spiritual directors and mechanics are not messiahs. These are simple, obvious observations.

Some unknown someone, long, long ago, separated life into two neatly divided compartments: the spiritual and the material, or the flesh and the spirit. This world and the next world were separated like night and day, as found in the expression, "East is East and West is West and never the twain shall meet!" That's why mechanics are never messiahs. The local folk of Nazareth were correct in asking the question about Jesus, "Isn't this the village carpenter?"

Religion and the world live separate lives, since most spiritualities are busily involved with rejecting "this world" in favor of the "next world." The very term "world" implies evil, power, corruption; while the term "spiritual" implies goodness, holiness and salvation. Naturally, then, these two never intermarry.

The Latin word for world, "saeculum," is the source of our word "secular." The secular is the direct opposite of the sacred. While the division of the spiritual and the secular has been the historical pattern for many a century, we must ask, "Is it still possible in our technological age? Can the spiritual continue to ignore the temporal or treat it as an enemy?"

Once, long ago, in simpler times, it was possible to turn one's back on secular-worldly concerns and go to the desert to be alone with God — to be separated

from the secular not for a few weeks, but for a lifetime. Entire peoples did this. They rejected "the world," packed up and went in search of a New Jerusalem. There, wherever they happened to be, they created a separate but holy culture, which was an island of the spiritual in a sea of the secular. We, however, are living in a temporal, secular world and in the midst of a non-religious culture. How, then, do we find a holiness that is whole and also in harmony with all of life?

Is it possible to neglect this modern world and still survive? Today, the ultimate catastrophic power is contained in our hands. We cannot reject that reality and seek holiness outside the secular. We cannot walk away from this world any more than we can walk away and turn our backs on a small child playing with a loaded pistol! We must find a secular spirituality instead of separating the secular realities from our way to God.

Yesterday's spiritual exercises often are as much out-of-date as yesterday's weather report. We need a contemporary spirituality that has incorporated the spiritual values of past ages with the complex realities of today. We need a modern pathway to holiness that will express our spiritual hungers as well as our secular work. We need a sacred-secular or secular-sacred liturgy for daily life! We need new prayer forms, new rituals and even new words to express this harmony of a sacred-secular life. Perhaps we may need some new commandments!

One possible new commandment could be, "You shall love the Lord your God with all your heart, with all your soul, and with all your strength; and you shall love the world as yourself!" Keeping this commandment will not be easy, for we will have to learn how to love this temporal world with a total heart. (When Scripture warns that we cannot love God and the world, "the world" means unloving and evil powers, not the or-

14

dinary, secular, daily world.) We will have to learn how to love the secular as we love our very selves. Think about it. Is it possible to love machines, computers, dirty laundry, taxes and all the unspiritual stuff that is a part of our daily life? Can we love our work, our professions, and, while doing so, see that this love is also a part of our love for God, the Divine Mystery?

When you love something, you take it seriously. We must learn not to neglect but to take seriously our mortgages, nuclear power plants, the use of chemicals, political elections, health care and events on a global scale. We already invest tremendous amounts of energy into these, but we see that expression as separate and apart from our love of God and our prayer life. While involved in a secular society, however, we have not lost our taste for the transcendental; we haven't forgotten our hunger for the sacred. But we need help to see the harmony and the holiness in all temporal things.

Churchy language and pulpit vocabulary doesn't help. The patterns of our worship and religious expression do not contain ideas like a holy carburetor, a blessed budget, a sacramental of separation or a prayer for paying taxes. One way to love the temporal would be to involve it in our ritual, to find ways to sacramentalize it, so we could express it symbolically as part of our way to God. But how?

Jesus, like Buddha and the other holy saviors, lived in the midst of deeply religious cultures. Jesus lived in a society that was overwhelmed with the presence of God, with the temple, religious ritual and prayer as the central focus of life. Yet, the Carpenter expanded the concept of the spiritual beyond a sacred society to all societies, even a secular society. His Way was that of the temporal, transformed and viewed from the inside, seen as a mystic contemplative would see it...alive with the Divine Mystery.

He gives us a pattern for how we can love the world and transform it. At his Last Supper, he takes ordinary, daily things – bread and wine – and while surrounded by ordinary folk, tax-collectors and fishermen, he transforms the secular into the divine. And why? Why take the temporal and transform it into the divine? *Love* was the reason! It was his love for his friends, his love for his Father and his love for the world that was the

reason for Jesus to invest himself totally into the temporal objects of bread and wine. Love has the magic, miraculous power to take the ordinary and to make it extraordinary.

But love the world? The world is too big to love. We mortals can only love that which we can put our arms around or hold in our hands. So this is where we must begin. We take that which fills our hands—our jobs, our work, our daily secular activities — and we transform them with love into ourselves! They will still smell like carburetors, still look and sound like IBM machines, but by our loving-prayerful touch they can become sacraments of ourselves and of our sacred-secular spirituality.

The new saints will be those who by their daily work, in the midst of a temporal technology, will sustain the world and so bring about its salvation. In their work they will find their nourishment as well as their prayer. As the ancient *Bhagavad Gita* of India says, "One reaches perfection by loving devotion to one's work."

To be a "new" saint will require knowledge and skill of one's work as well as the heart of an artist and lover. Such a heart is the same as that of a contemplative, since it can see beneath the chrome, steel and grubby realities of life to the internal mysterious presence. With a contemplative awareness, the work of the person becomes his art and his prayer. All work, as the Carpenter from Nazareth taught us, is holy, priestly, sacramental and worshipful. This awareness will only be possible if we are faithful to the commandment, "You shall love the Lord with all your heart, with all your soul, and with all your strength...and the world as yourself."

# Organic Reading:
# Teacher and Guide

What you are doing at this moment is reading. If you are like most of us, you arc in a hurry. Rcad slowly these instructions on "how to read." But, if you are able to read the instructions, you might ask, "Why do I need instructions on how to read?" Reading is a truly marvelous ability. It was one of the first skills we learned in grade school. The educational concept was simple but profound. Learn to read and then read to learn. Reading was the key to our entire education, both in school and in daily life.

In the Gospels, we read that Jesus went into the synagogue on Saturday, as was his custom, and that he stood up to read from the scroll of the prophet Isaiah. Like many other things in the Gospels, we can miss the marvels for the miracles. What is intriguing is that the village carpenter of Nazareth even knew how to read. We take that skill as ordinary and not the least unusual for an adult. But even today, in the closing years of the twentieth century, that ability to read is far from ordinary in many parts of this planet. In ancient days the skill of reading, as well as writing, was an art reserved for the temple priests. Even seven hundred years after Christ, the great emperor Charlemagne could not read or write. The monks that clustered about his throne were more than chaplains. They were his indispensable secretaries.

Today, while schooled in the skill, many people find it difficult to find the time to read. My sister-in-law once told me that to find time to read demanded

planning in her day. I am sure that many of you reading this have found it difficult to arrange your time so that some quiet and peace might be present. To read today for information or pleasure is not necessary, for we receive information and recreation from so many other sources. Messages come to us in a multitude of ways: television, radio, tapes, telephone, motion pictures, books, magazines, satellite communications and even the daily mail. The spiritual implications of these new transistorized sacraments have not yet been fully realized. The prophets of doom have, of course, labeled them as evil and dangerous, yet they can be tools for the construction of a New Jerusalem. Communications are the construction tools for the advent of the Kingdom.

These new means of communication, that have for many replaced reading, are tools for a new age, because they are shrinking the earth while expanding our personal worlds. Television alone makes us more catholic (universal). For example, during a twelve year period, international television transmissions by satellite increased from 80 to 13,000 hours a year. Those vast distances that once separated people from one another are shrinking at an unbelievable speed. The events in the lives of peoples on the other side of the world, peoples unknown to our grandparents, are now daily living room experiences. As we take part in this evolutionary miracle, we have to reshape our ideas and attitudes. We now enter into the mystery of good and evil on a global scale. As we do this, we shall need a new and global outlook on life, and we will need a new spirituality – a global spirituality.

You are interested in spirituality. If you were not, you would not even be reading this. You, like so many other people, seek some guidance and support for your inner life. As you look around for someone to guide you, the religious marketplace seems filled with those willing to be of service. From the Orient, gurus and

spiritual masters of all sizes and shapes offer to be your spiritual director. Bible-packing preachers and faith healers, together with Sunday morning TV evangelists, invite you to call upon them for help. With advent zeal, all these promise you direction in your faltering spiritual journey. But if every person who offered was truly competent, if every pastoral person you knew was willing and capable of giving spiritual guidance, there would still not be enough directors to direct everyone personally. Yet it seems some guidance is needed. Does not each person need some assistance in the pilgrimage to holiness? Perhaps personal, one-to-one direction is not absolutely necessary, though it may be of great value.

If you believe that the Divine Mystery is calling you, that the Divine Mystery is leading you, then God is your guru. As a guru, God is a perfect director since God knows the secret language of your heart. Perhaps you are, at this moment, being guided by your Spiritual Director – God. The primary function of a good spiritual director is simply to help the other listen to the heart. A good director always winds up out of business. Such a director furnishes the tools necessary for self-direction in the sense that the voice of the Divine Mystery can be followed alone. That voice speaks the messages needed for your personal journey. Down through the ages, there has always been a shortage of good spiritual directors, but there has never been a shortage of messages. Buddha was a message. Moses was another such message. Jesus is for some of us *the message,* not in microwaves but in flesh and blood. In fact, we have a global history of countless saintly satellites that have and are beaming "the message" to all who would take the time to listen, for all who take the time to read.

Today these "mystical messages" are interlaced in a web of communications. In 1980 the average American listened or was a spectator for about 50 hours

a week. That is a total of 2,700 hours a year, with television making up about eighty percent of that figure and radio the remainder. That same person read the newspaper for 215 hours a year and books for 175 hours a year. Reading as a skill is declining but still holding its own in a visual-spectator society. We can take heart that books are even being advertised on television! To lose the skill of reading would be more than a cultural loss; it would also be a personal and spiritual loss.

We seldom think or wonder about this skill that we learned in grade school. At this moment, you are

recognizing 200 to 300 printed symbols per minute, decoding those symbols into thoughts and ideas at the same flow as a conversation with the writer. A wondrous magical art is reading! Pre-media ages realized the great power in the printed word as an important tool in the religious life. Even today, surrounded as we are by a multitude of electronic message machines, reading remains a primary means for spiritual self-direction. Books, magazines, newspapers and articles can be for us that spiritual director we have been seeking.

The traditional name for such reading has been "spiritual reading." The very use of that term seems to imply that our lives are neatly divided into spiritual and secular. The marvel of *the message,* Jesus, was the incarnation (God becoming flesh). The incarnation proclaims a fact we have yet to fully live out, simply that the spiritual and the secular have been homogenized into one. Perhaps a better name for the reading we choose to do on our pilgrimage to wholesomeness is "organic reading." The organic is that which is related to growth, to life, to the ultimate purpose of existence, that which is integrated with the primary function of life. Unorganic reading is that hit-and-miss reading without a purpose. It is an activity to kill time in the dentist's office or to fill in time until our favorite program appears on television. Unorganic reading looks for no messages. The purpose of organic reading is related to the growth of the total person. Such reading is done with an attitude of mind that is open and constantly vigilant for messages. Unlike informational reading (the type we did in school), this reading does not seek knowledge but rather messages! The purpose and method of organic reading is based on the realization that once you have begun the pilgrimage to holiness, God will guide you with a continuous flow of messages. You are traveling on this pilgrimage to

wholesomeness as a cosmic amphibian, as a person both spirit and animal. We nourish the animal part of the amphibian in countless ways. You must also find ways to nourish the inner person and to awaken the intuitive part of the amphibian. Organic reading opens you to messages that can touch the unconscious. You will find such messages only if you are looking for them and only if you are reading the type of material that contains them.

To look for messages in reading is not easy since our training in that skill was primarily for the purpose of acquiring information. Remember the first grade lesson, "learn to read and then read to learn." Organic reading requires a different style if we are to find, and then decode, the messages that deal with our inner life.

Here are a few suggestions that may begin a process of thinking that will allow you to create your own techniques. First, it is not necessary to finish what you are reading before moving on to something else. It is not necessary to read only one thing at a time. You can read several writers at the same time. Since you are looking for messages, you may wish to read the material several times. Because you are not reading to meet a deadline, you can (and should) read much more slowly. You can set a pace that meets your needs – a page a day or a page a month. The speed of your reading should be such that you can leisurely allow yourself time for thought and prayer. Speed reading is actually opposed to organic reading, so your Evelyn Wood skills will be of little value to you in this area. Instead of speed, you need space. You need both inward and outward space (like reading in the bedroom with the door closed to the sounds of television and the playful noise of the children). You need the environment that will allow you to pause in your reading, to consider what you feel; the freedom to pause when something has touched you, to close the book and your eyes, and

24

reflect about what has been illuminated. Ask yourself the question, "What does this mean to me?" Pondering, you wonder how you can integrate the "message" into your daily life. Usually, you are able to receive and integrate only a single message at a time. Too many messages at the same time are not conducive to inner growth. This is the main problem with much of modern media: motion pictures, television and radio. While being extremely powerful stimuli, they do not allow for the person to stop the flow of images and ideas to explore a personal message that has been revealed. At best it seems that these "moving communications" can communicate a single overriding idea. The time to stop, the quiet to ponder and the leisure to expand a message are necessary if your reading is to be organic and to act as your guru.

> Ideally the pages of reading matter intended to be organic reading should have wide margins with ample room for writing. Ample margins allow space to pencil in your own thoughts, reflections and questions. Underscoring a thought and "fleshing out" an idea with your own thoughts is a way of entering into conversation with the writer. With a pencil as a prayer tool, you can write creatively your own commentary to the text. Now the book or magazine becomes an extension of you because you have personalized it. To then share it with another, especially if there is the freedom to pencil in comments, only increases its value.

An important technique in reading is what happens after you have finished reading. An effective way to activate the message is to discuss it with your friends or someone with whom you share the same spiritual

pathway. In that human and seemingly unproductive communion, words take flesh and ideas become reality. As you "mirror" the message of the reading to another person, that message becomes part of you as you express it in your own unique manner. Thoughts and ideas that are shared with others are ideas that become integrated. One of the main goals of organic growth is the creation of the *whole* person, a growth made possible by the integration of life and ideas.

An excellent question at this point would be, "Where do I find some organic reading material?" Naturally, sacred books are the prime containers of cosmic messages. Not only the sacred books of your religion, but all holy books contain truth. However, God is not restricted by copyright laws to holy books alone. Any reading can be organic, but usually it is found in those books, magazines or articles that deal with the needs of the inner person, with meditation and prayer. Reading that touches upon justice and peace, social attitudes and behavior and even the advancement of your life vocation is organic. Mindful that cosmic messages are simple in form but profound in meaning, you can look for them also in stories, parables and even science fiction. The letters of friends can be a marvelous medium for such messages. Organic reading is a reading that leads you closer to your final destination, to a sense of total unity and harmony. If you know where you are going in life, it will not be difficult to choose which reading material will be organic.

No matter what the source of your reading matter is, you must bring to it a sense of non-productivity if it is to be prayerful. For there will be times while reading when you will find no messages and no illumination. The words that you read then can be seeds that drop quietly into the unconscious area of the spirit and there sleep dormant for months and perhaps years. To the qualities of time, leisure and quiet, we now add

26

the next quality, patience, if you wish your reading to be your guru. The organic and prayerful reader allows for this process and does not push for productivity. You should take care that there is present within you an environmental openness so that such seeds can always find a fertile home.

Next, it is important to remember that some things you read will be hollow. It is not that they lack depth or substance; in fact, it is just the opposite – they are very "heavy" words. The composition of such words is like that of a lead pipe, hollow but heavy. Remembering the old spy movies when messages were often hidden in hollow canes, we lift these words out of the text. Carefully, we hold them and listen. Since they are hollow, God uses them to hide messages. They contain marvelous messages beyond the scope of the printed idea and even beyond the imagination of the original writer. To the list of qualities necessary to be a good reader, another quality may be added – a silence of heart is needed to listen for the messages hidden within the messages.

Faith is the last and most important quality needed if your reading is to be both prayer and spiritual direction. You, like Jesus when he read in the synagogue, must be possessed by a belief that a compassionate God wishes to speak to you. Such a faith will make you aware that it is not you who are taking a journey to God. Rather, you are being taken by God on a journey, and all necessary messages will come to you as you have need of them. With such an awareness, you will not walk in the footsteps of the great spiritual masters; instead you will seek what they sought, making your own path as you follow with faith the personal messages that come to you.

# Work: Blessing or Curse?

In Walt Disney's original version of *Snow White,* there is a charming scene where the Seven Dwarfs are trooping off to work. With picks and shovels on their shoulders, they march along in single file singing, "Hi Ho, Hi Ho, it's off to work we go!" Whistling a happy melody, they begin their day. As children, perhaps, we felt that it would be great fun to go off to work each day. But as we grew older and work became necessary for our livelihood, it was no longer looked upon as fun. Work was work and play was fun! Thus began that lifelong struggle between the demands of work and the desire for play.

As adults, a large part of our day is spent in work and not in play. We do not only have to make our daily bread, which doesn't grow on trees, but we must perform numerous tasks in the process of daily living that are also work – eating, dusting, caring for clothes, making our beds. Often, especially in our work-oriented society, these tasks are even more than work; they are chores that we dislike.

Even though work is important to us (Webster's dictionary has forty-one different listings under the word "work"), we often spend much time trying to escape from it! We may secretly dream of becoming millionaires so we can pay others to do our work. We may dream of winning some $100,000 sweepstake with the realization that then we could retire and live in luxury (the implication being that we would not have to work). Work can easily become a total way of life for

29

us. We can easily turn everything from our daily living habits to our profession into work. We can make a "project" out of everything, even brushing our teeth. In a society where our identification is linked to our work, that connection is much easier than we might think. Work is the curse of the sin of Adam. But is it really a curse?

Adam, our first parent, who didn't have to worry about doing any laundry, could be a patron saint for workers in a technological society. The writer of the Book of Genesis tells us: "The Lord God took the man (Adam) and put him in the garden of Eden to till it and care for it." Work, therefore, existed before the famous fall of Adam and Eve. After the fall, the natural act of work became a drudgery, but work itself is not a curse for the sin of Adam. Was Adam made to work, or was work one of the numerous gifts from our most generous God? If so, how is it a gift? Adam was occupied with the work of caring for his garden, which also happened to be God's garden, Eden. Here we have the first clue. His work was part of a much larger and more cosmic plan. His work was also done in communion with his Creator. Here it appears that Adam was also the first contemplative in our Western tradition, because he worked and lived in communion with his Creator. We do not find a single reference to Adam praying. Interesting, eh? The reason we do not is because Adam *was* prayer. His life was so intimately lived in harmony with creation, with the animals and plants and with his Creator, that everything was prayer. Adam was the first person to "pray always."

We are the great-great-great-grandchildren of Adam and Eve, and as a result we have also inherited, perhaps as part of our DNA code, that vocation to be contemplatives. We, too, should seek a lifestyle where our labor is our prayer, as well as all of life being prayer. George Bernard Shaw once wrote, "The purpose of

saints is not to edify us but to shame us!" The purpose of Adam, as the first saint, is to shame us into making our lives a harmony as was his and Eve's. We cannot leave our work, even simple household chores, out of our prayer lives and still call ourselves people who pray always. But how do we make our work, our daily activity, prayer?

First, we must attempt to enter into communion with what we do. We do this first by focusing our attention on the work of our hands. We discipline ourselves not to do two things at the same time. Try this and you will find it to be the most difficult of all forms of discipline. If we are digging a ditch, we dig the ditch and we do not let our minds work at something other than digging. The same applies to sweeping the floor, washing the dishes or taking a bath. A singleness of attention is essential for our work to be prayerful and enjoyable. Resist the efforts of the mind to be somewhere else, to be in the future or the past. Live in the present moment, and bring to that moment a keen sense of appreciation for what is happening.

Next, we seek a communion with the "stuff" of our work. We respect and reverence the wood, food, information, people, steel or whatever is the material of our work as we seek a communion with it. As we work in harmony with whatever touches our hands, we also see it as part of a cosmic continuation of creation. Like Adam, we are working with God, even in the most seemingly un-Godlike action. We work in harmony with time and do not try to force it to meet our needs. Adam lacked a pocket for a watch and followed a different style of time. As a result of having sunrise and sunset as key points in his day, he did not feel rushed to finish. Hurrying or rushing makes a sense of communion difficult. We must limit our activities so that we can do them with a sense of non-hurry. Most peo-

ple today are overworked, but that doesn't have to be the case. By learning to say "no" to others, to ourselves, perhaps to our compulsive need for accomplishment (to prove ourselves to others, or even to ourselves), we can limit the demands upon us.

Also, in his tilling the garden, Adam found a part of his identity but not the totality of that identity. What made Adam important was that he was Adam – not the

kind of work that he did. The same is true for any contemplatives. Their importance comes from being daughters or sons of God, not because of any title or job they do.

Next, we should strive to see that our work is a gift. Adam was living in paradise, yet he worked! God gave Adam work so that he might sense his harmony in the divine design. Work is a marvelous opportunity for us to build our well-being. By work we develop a relation-

ship between ourselves and others, and between ourselves and our talents. Work is a beautiful discipline for our little and limited egos. When we work with others and with creation, we must deal with our constant desire to be "in charge." Here was the place where Adam and Eve met their downfall; they desired not to be in harmony but to be in charge! Work with others forces us to control our need for constant self-centeredness. Work, like food, is essential for health of mind, body and spirit. But if our work is to nourish us (as it did Christ, for he said that his food was to do the work of the Father), it will need to be balanced with that other human activity of play or leisure. As Adam found a part of who he was in his work in the garden, we will also find a part of ourselves in our work. The other part is found in play. It is not impossible that our work can also be fun. In a large research laboratory of an American corporation, the director walks around and asks a single question of each scientist, "Are you having fun?" He feels that if his employees are having fun, that is, finding pleasure in their research, then great things will happen. The same is true with us. If our work is to be prayerful and nourishing, then it will be enjoyable. If we cannot find pleasure in what we do, we should perhaps change our attitudes or change our work.

If we enjoy our work, find fun in the challenge of it, we will no doubt do a good job. Excellence will be the result. Today, when so many of the products that we buy break down, we cannot but wonder if the people who made them found joy in their work. The loss of both excellence and a sense of pride is directly related to the loss of enjoyment in work.

The ancient Hindu and Christian method of liberation from attachment to things was to offer to God the success or failure, the fruit of our labors. When this sacrificial gift has been given, we can enjoy the very

act of work instead of its completion. It is much like swimming. The primary purpose of swimming is not to travel to the other side of the pool or lake, though that might be the case in some isolated occasion. The purpose of swimming is in the act of swimming. We find pleasure in getting wet, splashing around in water, one of the four sacred elements – earth, air, fire and water. We find pleasure in the exercise of our muscles, in the challenge of movement through water. So it should be in our work, when it is done in a sense of harmony. We find pleasure and prayer in our daily tasks, even cleaning our homes or preparing meals. Indeed, we will find times when our work is unpleasant and even difficult. Since we are still in the process of regaining the harmony lost by Adam in the Fall, we must be patient with ourselves at such times.

A hundred jobs will cry out to be completed, and the clock may shout that we have precious little time left, but if we can discipline ourselves to stop and sit still each day – in a time of silent prayer or meditation – we will learn the patience and the spirit of harmony necessary to pray always. Insofar as we are able to practice this simple prayer of daily stillness, of sitting still for fifteen or twenty minutes, we will soon know what is primary among all the tasks that face us. We will know that what is important is our relationship with God, ourselves and one another. We will then balance our work to include what is truly important with that which is fun.

When we find this balance, we will be able to rise above the guilt-producing judgments of others and also our own guilt feelings about work. Then we will find a life that can be lived wholly and joyfully in the present moment. It will be a life lived as a gift from God. The reward will be a new set of eyes and ears. We will also experience the privilege of enjoying our work, something that is becoming increasingly rare these
34

days. The Gospels tell us that the new Adam, Jesus, was a man who worked – that he was a carpenter. This work was not a preface to his ministry; it was a companion to his teaching and preaching. In Jesus we find the balance that Adam lost. For he had a profound awareness that his work was the Father's work and that he worked in constant communion with God. The words of Henry van Dyke so clearly express this:

<blockquote>
This is the gospel of labor,<br>
ring it, ye bells of the kirk!<br>
The Lord of Love came down from above,<br>
to live with the men who work;<br>
This is the rose that He planted,<br>
here in the thorn-curst soil;<br>
Heaven is blest with perfect rest,<br>
but the blessing of Earth is toil.
</blockquote>

Jesus, as a son of Adam and a son of God, was a contemplative. We should strive to be the same. As we attempt to make all we do, think and feel a communion with the divine, we will discover to our surprise that we are praying always.

First National
Bank & Trust Company

CASH | CURRENCY | 44 | 00
| COIN | | 89
LIST CHECKS SINGLY | |
RUSSELL | | 72 | 50
KETTER | | 130 | 00
| |
TOTAL FROM OTHER SIDE | |
TOTAL | | 247 | 39
CASH RECEIVED | | 50 | 00
DEPOSIT | | 197 | 39

For the love of money is the root of all evil.

COMMERCE BANK
CAPITAL & SURPLUS $50,000,000

# Love Your Money

Christianity has the reputation of considering sex as "dirty" and as the major hurdle to holiness. Second place for such dishonor must surely go to money — or, as it is called in the Bible, "filthy lucre" ("not greedy for filthy lucre" — 1 Tim. 3:3). Dirty sex and filthy money go together like Sodom and Gomorrha in our religious subconscious. Our disdain of money is heightened by the ugly fact that the first treasurer of the Church happened to be Judas Iscariot! While the Bible called money "filthy," have you ever heard of any church that refused to take a donation of the "dirty" stuff?

"It's a kind of spiritual snobbery," Albert Camus said, "that makes people think they can be happy without money." Are you and I spiritual snobs? Do you and I pretend that anyone can live like the "birds of the air" and still live in the world? Do we look with admiration on those few who have taken vows of poverty as living a higher life style because they don't have to handle money?

What did Jesus mean when he said, "You cannot give yourself to God and to money?" This and other remarks must be understood — but the question is, in what context? P.T. Barnum, the great American circus man, seems to sum up the attitude of Jesus when he said, "Money is a terrible master but an excellent servant." Jesus was concerned about those who make money their master and god, as in the "Almighty" Dollar. He was deeply concerned about the error, which is alive and well today, that money is the Giver of Happiness.

While Jesus looked upon neither sex nor money as filthy, it seems his later disciples did. We lack a constructive spirituality about either one of them. Not so with other religions!

Our word money comes from the name of the Roman goddess of money, whose temple was named Juno Moneta. In her temple, Roman money was coined. Juno was the wife of Jupiter and a rather busy goddess, being the patroness of women, war, virginity and marriage rites, as well as of warnings — hence the Latin word for warning, "monere." Clever idea that our word "money" stems from that root and that the goddess of money was also the giver of warnings! Jesus would have liked that.

While past Christian religious attitudes may have looked down on money as being outside the realm of spirituality (except when one gave it to the Church), the reality of life is that we can't live without it. Money is a necessary medium of transaction for those living in a complex civilization. Primitive peoples were able to barter ("I'll give you two fish for a basket of corn"), but that isn't possible today as a general norm. Interestingly, our slang word for dollar, "buck," comes from the barter system. Between 1700 and 1750 a quarter of a million to half a million buckskins were traded each year on the American frontier. By 1850 the term "buck," meaning "dollar," was well known. Money — a buck, bread, jack, moola, cash or by any other name — is a central part of our lives, and therefore deserves to be part of our spirituality. And because money is itself a symbol, the surprise is that it can easily share in the world of religious attitudes and ideas, a world of symbol, sign and sacrament.

The money in our billfolds or pocketbooks, in our checking or savings accounts, is first of all a symbol of ourselves. Samuel Butler said, "Money is the symbol of duty; it is the sacrament of having done for man-

kind that which mankind wanted."

Butler's idea of money as a sacrament may take a little time to be convincing to us because our prejudice and disdain runs so deeply. However, we receive money from the work we have done; therefore it is a symbol of ourselves. After barter became impossible, token objects were exchanged instead of goods or produce. Around 1000 B.C. metal money appeared in China. The Chinese first made it of bronze and in the shape of little spades, knives and other tools. This early form of money not only represented the objects originally used in barter but was also a symbol of the work of such tools.

Paper money, and even more a paper check, is far removed from such rich symbolism, so it is easy for us to forget that our money is a symbol of our work. Since we are not filthy, why should we regard our symbol, money, as "unclean"? Indeed, Scripture says that "the love of money is the root of all evil" (1 Tim. 6:10), but does not Jesus tell us to love our neighbor as we love ourselves? Logically it would seem that we could say, "Love your money as you love yourself — since it is a sacred symbol of yourself." The person who is a tightwad and "squirrels" away his money usually is also uptight, and finds it difficult to be generous, outgoing and expressive. And those who throw away their money on drink and drugs usually end up by throwing themselves away as well. What you do with your money says a great deal about who you are and what you value.

In the apostolic community of the early Church we are told that the early Christians "shared all things in common; they would sell their property and goods, dividing everything on the basis of each one's needs...with exultant and sincere hearts they took their meals in common" (Acts 2:44-46). Their sharing of their money could not be separated from their sharing of

39

themselves and their prayers and meals. But a good $pirituality also should contain a warning, in memory of the Goddess of Money and in light of the cautionary words of Jesus.

The symbol or sign of our basic medium of exchange, the dollar, is this $. The source of this symbol, it is believed, came from the Spanish Piece of Eight. The "S" part of the sign is a broken 8, the two vertical bars that stand over it may represent the two "Pillars of Hercules" that were on the back side of that Spanish coin. "The Pillars of Hercules" is the name the ancients gave to the two giant rocks that stood on either side of the Strait of Gibraltar, the entrance from the Mediterranean to the Atlantic Ocean. So on those Spanish Pieces of Eight, that entrance was symbolized by two pillars bound together by a scroll on which was written "Ne Plus Ultra." The inscription means "No More Beyond," and was given to sailors as a warning not to go out into the Atlantic. Beyond the Pillars of Hercules, lay only great monsters of the deep, terrors beyond imagination and death itself!

Jesus, when talking about money, seems to caution us, " 'Ne Plus Ultra'...No More Beyond!" Money is only a symbol; nothing of value exists beyond its face value unless we learn how to invest it as a sacrament of ourselves and of the Kingdom. Surprisingly, the Gospel is full of financial advice! When the Gospels talk (as the famous E.F. Hutton commercial says), people should listen. That advice is about obtaining invisible and non-perishable wealth; how to become a mystic millionaire! We are challenged to invest both ourselves and our money in a way that will make us truly wealthy people. But as every Wall Street speculator knows, high dividends are made only from investments that have high risks. Play it safe with your investments, and you will hardly keep up with the rate of inflation.

Daily, you and I encounter opportunities to invest
40

our time and talents as we invest our money. If we give ourselves only to the NOW, investing only in our own physical needs, pleasures and desires, we invest in something with no risk. We have an immediate return for our investment of money. When we use our money only for ourselves or "squirrel" it away, we should remember the sailor's warning at the gates of Hercules, "No More Beyond!" But just as Columbus found a whole new world beyond the Straits of Gibraltar, so we also can find a whole new and holy world beyond the face value of our dollars.

A $pirituality of money could begin with some guidelines:

(a) First, we should love our money and take pride in it. It is good to be proud of having earned it, for money is one sign of a job well done. Every paycheck is a pat on the back.

(b) Next, mindful that our money is a sacrament in which we can say, "This is me...this is my sweat and toil...," we should use it to nourish our bodies, which it represents. So, part of our income goes for food, clothing, shelter and also for entertainment and fun. This expression of self-love is good and holy.

(c) The dollar bills in your billfold are not only a sign of you, but also of the community to which you belong. They are the frequent reminder that you belong to a certain nation whose money you use symbolically. So, with part of your money you pay taxes. You should rejoice that this communion of self helps to build highways, pay teachers' salaries and patch up the potholes in the street in front of your house. (I realize that part of your tax dollar also is spent on deadly military weapons, but that is an issue too complex to deal with in this chapter.) Each year at IRS time you could pray a prayer to Saint Matthew, the tax collector whom Jesus called to be one of the twelve: "Saint Matthew, Holy Tax Collector, help me to see in my

41

taxes a gift of myself to my country, my state, county and township. In justice may my money serve those with whom I live in community; may I not resent this duty that is mine. Amen."

(d) Some of your money goes into our Social Security system and is given to the elderly and the needy. So, a part of you puts food on the plate of some aged man or woman or helps pay the rent of an elderly person. By means of this withholding payment you are able to put flesh on the words that Jesus speaks about seeing him in those who are in need.

(e) Now, an important part of any spirituality is a sense of play. As Alan Watts said, "I am sincere about prayer, but I never take it seriously!" While finance is serious business, we shouldn't take money seriously! In the early days in Canada, it seems that the colonials ran out of French money. So, the first appearance of paper money in the New World was their temporary solution to that problem. The Canadians took playing cards, assigned certain values to them, and then the colonial French governor signed each of them. Even after the "real" money arrived from France, they continued to use this Play Money for over 70 years. Maybe it was more fun — certainly it was more colorful. A pattern for such playfulness might be found in recalling the times when we played the game of Monopoly. When we lost our hotel on Park Place and a bankroll as well, the world did not come to an end...it was just a game. One time the cards would hold a huge gas bill to pay, the next time it would be a gift in the will of Aunt Nellie. Perhaps it would be well to transfer some of the light-heartedness of that play money to our use of real money. In so doing we should be mindful of the promise of Jesus that cancels our anxiety about the future, "Seek first the Kingdom and everything you need will be given to you."

(f) Finally, in numerous ways we are inclined to

use parts of our money on gifts to those we love, to friends and to those organizations and activities we feel are important to the world and to growth of the human spirit. Whenever we give a gift of money we could seal it with a kiss or a wink...saying, "This is my body...this is me...this is my love."

This chapter about $pirituality is but a small beginning at the task of creating an attitude that incorporates our money and daily life with our prayer and worship. May it be a "starter" for your own thoughts and ideas. As Richard Armour once said, speaking for us all,

That money talks
I'll not deny,
I heard it once:
It said "Good-bye."

As we bid farewell to our dollars, let us begin our $pirituality by sending each of them away with our own blessing of love upon all who receive them.

# Home-Church-Shrine

In his book *The Brook Kerith* George Moore wrote, "A man travels the world over in search of what he needs and returns home to find it." We do not find the mystic doorway to the Sacred in far-off Tibet or at some ancient shrine; it dwells within our homes. Anglo-Saxons have an old saying that our homes are our castles. As we come to the end of the twentieth century we are beginning to discover that our homes are *temples,* our personal sacred spaces. Those places where we live are first of all more than shelters; they are mirrors of ourselves. Our homes reflect our tastes, our interests and what we value. If God is an integral part of our lives, then the Divine Mystery should also find a dwelling place in that space we call "home." God becomes an intimate companion in the lives of spiritual seekers. Where then does this Divine Roommate dwell within our homes?

We know that the entire cosmos is God's house. But when God is everywhere, God is nowhere. Long ago, when all of creation was viewed as sacred, our parents realized that sacred space was essential to awaken them to the sacredness of all space. Indeed, the human heart is *the* temple of the Holy, but earthpeople also need to have some tangible sign of the invisible Presence. Public sacred places were first sacred shrines in nature – a mountain, a grove of trees, a river. These then were followed by stone circles, pyramids and temples. Each home also had its house shrines to the gods or family ancestors.

45

To create a sacred space in the home, then, is nothing new or novel; in fact, it is a most ancient practice. Before the age of churches and cathedrals, every home had its shrine. We also know that in the first three centuries of Christianity the communal celebrations of the death and resurrection of Christ, the memorial meal of his Last Supper, took place in the homes of believers. Today, then, when we set aside space for prayer and worship in our homes, we are only returning to our primal religious roots.

In the typical twentieth century home there are special rooms set aside for the important activities of our lives; rooms in which to sleep, eat, wash, relax, study, do the laundry, park the car and pursue our crafts and hobbies. We have little rooms, closets, to house our clothing and life equipment. It only seems logical that, if our life's journeys imply a companionship with the Divine Mystery, this Mystery should have a special space as well.

Ideally this sacred space should be an entire room, even if it is only as large as those rooms where we store our clothing. But when this is not possible, surely a small corner could be set aside as a shrine. This space is first of all a reminder that the entire home is sacred, and everything that takes place within it is a holy and integral part of our inner quest.

The house shrine is the place for meditation and prayer and a place to keep personal relics. Each time we pass it we are reminded that the search for sanctity is an everyday affair. By its presence we are called to the necessity of prayer as the language of daily reverence for the workaday pilgrim. A prayer corner within the home can remind us of the three holy places in every home: the threshold, where the ritual of hospitality is performed; the table, where we celebrate the mystery of the meal; and the bedroom, where we nightly perform the dress-rehearsal of "falling asleep"

46

to awaken to the Eighth Day. The bedroom is also, for many seekers, the holy place for the ritual of reunion, the sacrament of love. Indeed, all three of these are places where human love is celebrated as holy; they become the classrooms for learning how to love the mystery of God enfleshed in our world.

Setting aside a home shrine is clear evidence of the belief that God is not an "only-on-Sunday" experience. One reason why shrines are absent in today's homes is that in our secular society we tend to hide our spirituality. It is not because we are likely to be persecuted, but because public religious expression is considered to be in bad taste. We fear that we might appear fanatic or be thought to belong to a "lower" or immigrant class. "Educated, sophisticated adults" do not have need of such religious values. So, we have tended to remove our sacred signs from the central area of our homes to more private areas as a means of escaping ridicule and the possible criticism of being "simple" or lacking in culture. But the shrine, whether in a central room or a consecrated corner, is an open gateway to the deeper meaning of life, no matter what the current fashion is.

Long ago in China, Confucius said, "The strength of a nation is derived from the integrity of its homes." Our lives lack integrity when they are devoid of the presence of the Divine Mystery as a part of daily life. Much of the poverty of today's organized religions is due to the fact that the daily life of most people has been cut off from prayer, meditation, ritual and a sense of cosmic celebration. The structures called churches were never intended to be the sole places to house the holy. When churches are cut off from their source of prayerful energy – the home – the sense of the sacred within their walls is threatened.

Christianity is not a religion; it is a way of life. In a religion it is proper to perform certain duties and to

take upon ourselves certain moral obligations and beliefs. But a Way of Life affects every aspect of daily life – from business to bathing, from sleeping to sweeping the floor. A secular sanctity is a "home-made" holiness, where the profane and common are seen with an inner vision that transforms them into prayer. This does not mean that we need to make our homes look like churches but rather that we elevate the ordinary objects and aspects of life to the realm of liturgy – to worship. When we begin to do this in our homes, it is not long before we invest the other activities and places of our lives with the same sense of the sacred wedded to the secular. But we cannot hope to make our work place, or the world itself, "alive with God" if our homes are empty of the holy. And as we become accustomed to sharing a meal or an act of affection in our homes as a form of worship, it becomes easier to do so in public, in the desert of today's secular society.

To see the human events of our existence as sacred requires a contemplative attitude. That effort can only arise from a constant effort to sanctify every action with prayer and attention. It is then that we begin to raise a tabernacle of glory, a tent of the holy, over the various events of our lives. The times when we act with love and creativity, when we find pleasure and enjoyment, become for us like the roadside table on the road to Emmaus. You will recall how the two disciples of Jesus, after his death, while breaking bread at a supper meal, suddenly became overwhelmed with the presence of Christ at their table. The space between them, a space set with bread, wine, some fish and salt, became as sacred as the Holy of Holies of the Temple in Jerusalem. When we make it possible for the Divine Presence to enter the common events of our home life, we will discover that the Sacred Mystery will appear to us at the countless crossroads of life with increasing ease and frequency. As the home becomes a shrine,

so will the cosmos once again become a temple – and all that we do within it will be worshipful.

So let us begin to create a place for the Holy to be manifest in our living quarters. We might place a sacred image such as an icon or cross in the corner of a bedroom. A rock or block of wood is adequate for an altar, the most primitive of all signs of God. Before it might lie a small rug used only for prayer, which when we travel can be rolled up and taken, along with a sacred image, to make a portable shrine for a hotel room. The shrine can also have its tabernacle, a container which holds the precious objects of our journey in life: a pebble, a love letter, a relic of a parent's devotion or the relics we have gathered from holy places. Ritual patterns are enhanced by the use of a candle, incense and flowers. According to each person's taste, the shrine, like the rest of the home, takes on the personality of its priestly owner.

The home shrine is the natural beginning and closing place of our day. We come to it to meditate, to pray in times of sorrow and great need or to give thanks for events that cause the heart to dance. When time is short, we can pause for a moment, simply standing in silence before the shrine, allowing its power to wash over us and refocus our hearts as we rush from event to event. When life turns against us and anger or frustration rises up within, we can retreat to our sacred space and draw strength from that meeting with the Mystical. Then we can return, balanced and at peace, to face our issues with an insight that heals and restores. Indeed, the strength that sustains us is not found in the world, but rather in our homes and in our hearts. We need only the discipline to seek the treasure where it is hidden.

Finally, those who make their homes and daily lives sacred will find that they are enriching religion! The saying of Confucius could be paraphrased, "The

strength of *religion* is derived from the integrity of its homes." As you find the deep fountain of holiness in your heart and in the ordinary events of life, you will bring that sense of the sacred to the world and to religion. When you then pray or worship with others, you will enrich them as the energy of your life of prayer flows outward to elevate the corporate worship. Today churches need this gift more than gifts of money or time served on committees. The home shrine is not a retreat from communal church activities but is rather an essential element in their revival, for no one goes to heaven alone. We are a corporate people, and we struggle together to rise to a new level of consciousness, a Christ-consciousness. The shrine in the home is an important springboard for that communal "coming home" to God.

# The Primal Sacrament

Not only our home but our hospitality has spiritual aspects. Prayer is possible anywhere and at any time. When we hear the word "prayer," we at once think of church or synagogue. However, the church is but the historical development of the primal church, which is the home. The home or the "domestic church" was the place of prayer, sacrifice, worship and spiritual life. The parish church or your local church is intended to be the communal gathering of the domestic churches that surround it. When our homes cease to be domestic churches, then the vitality of the local church is short-lived.

Anywhere in the home is proper for prayer, but three places stand out as cardinal points – the table, the bedroom and the threshold. The first two appear as simply natural, but the third may not at first glance seem that logical. What kind of prayers could you pray at your front door?

The prayer of the front door is one of the most universal and ancient of all prayers, and its name is hospitality. Actually it is more than simple prayer, for it is the first sacrament and as such is worship. We who live in a non-spiritual culture consider the door of a home to be a necessity, but our ancient ancestors considered it as a holy place and a sacred shrine. To believe today that the threshold of your home is a shrine might be considered quaint. To consider the most common, daily actions like saying "hello" and "good-bye" as prayerful and holy deeds would be thought of as odd. Yet,

53

to invite friends to dinner or to receive an invitation to enter another's home is held sacred by all peoples. Or rather, it was held to be sacred prior to our age of progress.

In former ages, people believed that the gods, hidden in disguise, came to visit as strangers. This belief is not restricted to one or two religions but is held by almost all of them. As a result, hospitality was considered as a prime religious requirement. In the Scriptures we find numerous references to the extraordinary stature of guests. Abraham, Tobias, Lot and their families entertained guests with honor and respect, only to find that they had indeed entertained God! Paul expressed one of the teachings of the early Christian community on hospitality when he said, "Do not neglect to show hospitality, for by that means some have entertained angels without knowing it" (Heb. 13:2).

In Jewish spirituality there was a saying: "Hospitality to strangers is greater than reverence for the name of God!" Considering the profound reverence for the name of Yahweh, we can gather how awesome is what happens at the front door. We are familiar with the sound of church bells as a call to prayer and worship. The sound of the doorbell also calls us to prayer, a worship that demands greater reverence than pronouncing the name of God. The doorbell or the knock at the door is indeed a call to prayer and an invitation to the sacrament of care of the stranger. As a sacrament it has cosmic dimensions. The Hebrews, Chinese, Greeks, Romans and all ancient peoples considered guests as sacred; they also reverenced the common comings and goings of the family. The threshold of the home was a holy place, the sanctuary of these daily comings and goings. As such it has been protected by a variety of guardian spirits.

On the doorpost of a Jewish home is placed the Mezuzah. In keeping with the command of Moses that

the Word of God should be inscribed upon the doorpost of the home, a small box or container is placed there. Inside is a hand-scribed quotation from the Torah which contains the name of God, El-Shaddaei, the All Holy One. This Mezuzah is a protection for the home from evil and a constant reminder of the sacred nature of the threshold. The prayer custom is to touch the Mezuzah and then kiss the fingertips upon entering and leaving the home.

The pre-Christian Romans assigned a special god named Janus to guard and bless the doorway. He had two faces so that he might watch the front and back doors at the same time. The god Janus was the custodian of welcoming and bidding farewell to guests and strangers. As you may have already guessed, his name was given to the doorway month of the year, January! Those persons who had as their special duty the care of the threshold were called, after his name, janitors, and less common today, janitresses. The janitor was the minister of the sanctuary of the door, not merely someone who kept the house clean.

According to Moslem spiritual theology, on the day of judgment we must all give a full account of what we have done with the time and money that God has given us. God will demand a full accounting of these two important talents. But, it is said, God will never ask about money or time used in hospitality. So sacred is that action that God would be ashamed to inquire about it. The contemporary person might easily smile at such primitive theology, or the belief that the gods and goddesses come to us as strangers, or that shaking hands is prayerful worship. But remember that our expression "good-bye" is a relic of that age and a reminder of our amnesia about the true nature of hospitality. Once, a long time ago, "good-bye" was said much more slowly, and it sounded like "God be with you."

We also remember that Jesus was a wandering
55

teacher-rabbi and his followers had a wandering ministry that also made hospitality a necessity. "Whatsoever you do to the least of my brethren, you do unto me...I was a stranger and you took me in...." Each of us then is called to be a janitress or a janitor as we become holy ministers of the threshold. In the words of the early Christian community, "Be generous in offering hospitality." The issue, then, was more than hospitality as a necessity, for that expression was an important part of a living spirituality. That relationship between hospitality and the inner life remains interlocked even today.

Prayer and the care of guests, of the stranger or friend, are expressions of the divine flow in the universe. Prayer is an awareness, an attitude of remembering, that we are all guests in this world. Prayer is an expression of gratitude for the ways in which we are entertained, gifted and loved by the divine host. Hospitality is but one way to continue the divine flow of gifts through us to others. When we fail to be grateful, to lift up our hearts in gratitude, according to the ancient holy ones, the divine flow ceases. Deeds of kindness and courtesy, of welcoming and friendship, are ways to allow the gifts of life that have come to us to flow on out into the world and to return to their original source. Hospitality has implications beyond polite manners because our capacity for receiving is linked to our ability to give. The closed hand and heart that are unable to give love are also unable to receive love.

Within the universe is a stream of divine energy, a sacred flowing of life and love. The divine love is constantly giving itself in an endless stream of daily gifts as God flows out of God and into the world. We discover these flowing gifts in the daily experiences of life by which we are loved. We then pass them onward to others so that this love might return to its source,

56

the divine heart of God, only to begin its journey all over again. This divine flow is mirrored in the cosmic plan within the cycle of rain. Water is constantly moving from the heavens to earth and returning again. Unlike water, the flow of love can stop at the human heart. We can trap the gifts and keep them for ourselves and never pass them on. We each possess the power to close the doors of our hearts and stop the flow. The human heart has a door that closes more easily than it opens. However, the divine flow of gifts freely comes to us, and freely it must pass through us on its mystic journey back again to the divine source.

By deeds of hospitality this flowing return of gifts continues as we attempt to love others without seeking profit. As the Teacher said, "When you entertain do not only invite your friends but also the poor and the outcast because they will be unable to repay you by an invitation to their homes." We should seek those opportunities to keep the flow of gifts moving through the universe. Each day we are presented with expressions of God's love in the beauty of creation that surrounds us and in acts of kindness and affection. We are also provided daily with numerous means of allowing this love to return to its source. Kindness to the stranger can be expressed not only at the threshold of our homes but at the ten thousand other doorways of life. Daily we encounter the stranger (most of whom we may not see again) as clerks in stores, business people and service persons, as well as travelers on the road. In all of these doorways we should be mindful of their sacred nature and also mindful of the flow of divine love that is on its way back again to God.

At these countless doorways of life, as well as at your own front door, is found a trinity of the threshold – reverence, love and sincerity. Sincerity is of absolute necessity in hospitality since nothing interrupts the divine flow as does dishonesty. Insincerity

is that divorce between what we think or feel and what we say and do. All pretending is alien to true prayer. If we cannot be sincerely kind and reverent, then it is better not to open our front doors. Better that we stay "closed-in" than that we act with dishonesty. If we are unable at this moment to give ourselves to others for various reasons, what better reminder is there that we have closed the doors of our hearts than to hide behind our closed doors and pretend that we are not at home? That refusal to come to our doors is more honest than to open our doors and pretend that we are courteous and loving. All dishonesty is dangerous, if not lethal, to the growth of the inner life.

Because both love and reverence require time, we should not be surprised at their recent absence from modern life. Today our two most precious possessions are time and money. Should we be surprised that we find a void of prayer and reverence in our homes, as well as a lack of hospitality, since we live in a "hurry up" and "rush-rush" society? Being always busy prevents other natural virtues from being present in our homes. We need not only time but also faith to handle persons and things with reverence. We need a living belief that *the* reality of all life does exist beneath the most ordinary and common things.

Time and faith are not sufficient in themselves to revive love as part of the trinity of the threshold. Love has been replaced in our world not by hate so much as it has been suppressed by fear. We are afraid to be kind to the stranger! We are afraid to exchange the normal courtesy, for in the process we might be robbed or raped. The contemporary news media daily give us a blow-by-blow account of crime and terrorism. This continuous coverage of crime as news has had its deadening effect — and what has died is hospitality to the stranger. So easily we forget that for each act of terror there are ten thousand acts of tenderness

(hospitality) that will never find their way into the daily
paper or the news program. As a result, welcome mats
are rolled up and stored away in the back of the basement. We buy more and more locks for our front doors
and, sadly, for our hearts as well. Tu Fu, a wandering
poet of the eighth century in China, expressed his concern at a rebellion in the city of Ch'ang-an by a bar-
barian general with the lines:

> The rustic old fellow from Shao-ling
> weeps with stifled sobs,
> as he walks furtively along the bends
> of the Serpentine River on a spring day;
> In the palaces by the river front
> the thousands of doors are locked
> For whom have the fine willows and new rushes
> displayed their fresh green colors

60

Has not the fate of the citizens of Ch'ang-an behind their locked doors also become our fate? Has not fear prevented us from experiencing the fine willows as well as the fine people of the world?

Indeed, we all need to be cautious as well as prudent for a growing crime rate is a reality, but so is the presence of God in the stranger a reality. We have a need to control the growing anxiety that feeds our childhood apprehension of the stranger. This anxiety which causes us to treat persons like things is fed also by our entertainment. When our entertainment is focused on robbery, murder and violence, the fear grows. As a result, we today, unlike the ancient ones, see not a god but a demon in the stranger! Somehow we need to rediscover the beauty and grace in hospitality.

The rebirth of the sacrament of hospitality can begin not with the stranger but among the very persons with whom we live or work. Here in the daily encounters of life, in the comings and goings, in meals and shared activities, we need reverence, sincerity and love for each other. We need to recapture the mindfulness that expressions like "good morning" and "good night" are prayerful blessings. We need to remember that common actions like opening a door, fetching a cool drink and saying "hello" are prayers and sacramental deeds. If we treat all these common family and communal acts as holy, surrounding them with reverence and sincerity, we will never have to fear that we will treat a stranger or guest with disrespect.

# Prayer and the Bathroom

There is a line in a Vietnamese folk song well worth some serious thought: "Hardest of all is to practice the Way at home, second in the crowd, and third in the pagoda." That folk song has a universal ring about it; how true it is! As we look around our homes, which room is the hardest in which to practice the Way? Correct; the answer is the bathroom! We do not find it difficult to pray in the living room, the dining room or even the bedroom, but does anything prayerful ever happen in the bathroom? Indeed, our homes can be called "domestic churches," but it seems that we can easily leave out that one room from the consecration.

Since it moved indoors, the toilet has joined forces with the bathtub-shower and wash basin to create the contemporary bathroom. What we call this part of the home tends to reveal how we feel about it. Look at a few of the euphemisms, the inoffensive names, we have for this one room: bathroom, powder room, jakes and restroom. (This last name is especially humorous because of the lack of comfortable furniture or time to rest there.) The British call bathrooms lavatories, a word sounding very much like laboratories. And, for a while, they resembled laboratories — white, sanitary and sterile. Institutional bathrooms still maintain this sanitary, sterile environment.

Except in the homes of movie stars or the very rich, bathrooms have tended to be small, cramped rooms usually devoid of artistic beauty and warmth. Decorators and architects have recently attempted to

make them more pleasant and cheery – the sort of places one would enjoy spending time. But the addition of green plants, natural woods, larger windows and carpeted floors has not necessarily helped us to find them any more prayerful or to think of them as shrine-rooms. The bathroom in every home is essential to modern sanitation, but what does it have to do with modern sanctification? Most would answer that question by saying, "Bathrooms are for cleanliness and sanitation; churches are for inspiration and sanctification."

But is this necessarily the case? Edmund Wilson, American writer, literary and social critic, said, "I have had a good many more uplifting thoughts, creative and expansive visions – while soaking in comfortable baths or drying myself after bracing showers – in well-equipped American bathrooms than I ever had in any cathedral." Though the bathtub or toilet is hardly the place where one might expect "expansive visions," an experience that I had one summer when I was a college student, suggested that it might be otherwise. I worked for the Kansas City street department, and the driver of the truck to which I was assigned was a black, self-educated Baptist minister. Knowing that I was studying to be a priest, he told me of how God had called him to the ministry. He said that it had happened in the bathroom! At age 19, I thought that extremely strange and rather humorous. But now at 53, and a wee bit wiser, I consider it to be not only natural but beautiful. The bathroom, of all the rooms in our homes, has many possibilities for prayer, visions and divine calls.

Bathrooms are "enchanted" places, rich in creativity and fertile for inspiration, as Edmund Wilson knew. Remember that the famous Greek mathematician and inventor, Archimedes, discoverd the priciple of buoyancy (hydrostatics) while taking a bath. The bathroom is
64

the one place where we daily come into bodily contact with water – that mystic, sacred element that existed together with God before creation. As the writer of Genesis tells us, "In the beginning when God created the heavens and the earth...a mighty wind swept over the waters." Water, that essential substance of baptism, has its shrine in our bathrooms. As you slip into your bathtub after a long, hard day, you may find that it is also a place of prayer. The steam, like the smoke of incense, ascends slowly from the water. As it rises, it carries with it all aches and pains, the burdens of the day and the echoes, hidden in your skin, of the frantic rushing of the day. When we are freed from distracting impediments, we are much more ready, responsive, to meet God face to face. All such preparations are prayers in themselves.

The real issue is not how to make our bathrooms places of prayer, but rather of acknowledging that they already are! Many of us have already found them to be places of spontaneous, natural prayers that appear on our lips. An example is the grateful sigh for a good bowel movement after a time of constipation, or the words of praise as we feel the glow of a brisk towel rub after an invigorating shower. We don't tell people about this secret prayer-place or of our experiences there. Perhaps if we spoke about them, people might call us heretics or think us strange.

The prime reason for calling the bathroom a place of prayer is that it is the one place in the home where we can be guaranteed privacy (except for mothers with toddlers). Once the door is closed, we have our own desert, hermitage and hide-out – the precious space in which to be alone. George Bernard Shaw, no fan of America, said, "An American has no sense of privacy. He does not know what it means. There is no such thing in the country." Wrong, Mr. Shaw! We do have privacy in our crowded lives, and it is found in the smallest

65

room in the house. In the average, hectic household, where else can you go to be totally alone? Eleanor Roosevelt went into the bathroom to cry, turning on the water taps full force to cover the sound of her weeping. It was the one place where she could release without embarrassment the pent-up emotions of her life. Haven't you, at one time or another, sought refuge in the restroom? Behind its closed door, you could cry, grit your teeth or muster up your courage to look in the mirror as you talked yourself into being more dynamic or patient or understanding.

Here in Kansas there are still a few outhouses, also known as *privies*. This delightful names means "secret" or "private," as in the term "Privy Council." And, recall that when Jesus gave instructions on how to pray, he said, "When you pray, go to your room, close the door, and pray to your Father in private" (Mt. 6:6).

While all this may make good sense, the question remains, "Why is the bathroom the least talked about place of prayer?" The bathroom is not only the place where we bathe or cleanse ourselves, it is also the place where we move our bowels and care for the eliminations of the body. And we associate guilt, shame and a host of hidden negative feelings with such functions, making this one room out-of-bounds for blessedness.

A variety of social and religious taboos surround the body, especially the sexual organs. Who is responsible for these taboos and for the guilt we associate with the body? The Church? The clergy? The modern Church only points the finger of blame back to the Puritans. And they in turn would say, "No, not us, the villains are the Manichaeans." Indeed, the guilt might be placed at the feet of the Manichaeans, a heretic sect of the early Church which taught that matter is evil, that the body is evil. But they might claim innocence and point further back to Moses and the Book of Leviticus.

The Jews at the time of Leviticus were a cultic peo-

ple whose lives were deeply involved with their God Yahweh. They were extremely concerned about ritual cleanliness; there is a long list of what was thought to make a person unclean. Sexual functions which involved the touch or loss of semen made one "unclean" because of the loss of vitality. One was unclean for a day, and then it was necessary to bathe. Childbirth and

menstruation made a woman "unclean" because of the loss of blood, which to primitive peoples was "life." Besides these, to touch a dead body also made one "unclean." The ritual uncleanliness of such acts separated the person from others and from worship but had nothing to do with their morality. Such causes for cultic unworthiness were not unique to the Jews but were common among primitive peoples. However, the

use of such terms like "unclean" led easily to attitudes of "dirty" when referring to our sexuality and bodily functions.

Birth, sexual love and death all have one thing in common that has caused some scholars to offer another opinion about their being "unclean" – one that gives new importance to the bathroom as a holy place. Two persons sharing sexual love were seen as acting in communion with God in creating life. Birth and death were also sacred times when the hand of God was upon a person. If in sex and death one is touched by God, then one is made holy by such a touch. Therefore, the need to be separated from others, to wash, according to the view of some, is the need to remove "holiness" before returning to a profane world! In addition, semen and urine have also been viewed as sources of life, healing and blessing. Hence there is an old European custom of treating impotence by urinating through the wedding ring. Even more interesting is the custom of a Hottentot wedding ritual in which the priest urinates on the bride and groom! Science has confirmed the healing properties of urine, which primitive peoples already seemed to know. Urokinase, derived from human urine assists the body in the removal of blood clots. These "unclean" parts of the human experience can thus be viewed in a different light.

Jesus, furthermore, uses his most severe words to condemn what was behind the need for ceremonial washing as required by the Law. All is holy, all is life, and so there is no need for the division of sacred and profane. The human body is to be viewed as Jesus viewed his own body – as a temple. Henry Thoreau said as much in *Walden:* "Every man is the builder of a temple, called his body, to the god he worships, after a style purely his own, nor can he get off by hammering marble instead. We are all sculptors and painters, and our material is our own flesh and blood and bones."

68

In various religious traditions the saying of ritual prayers of cleansing has helped to raise this consciousness. Among devout Jews, for example, there is the tradition of the Berakhot prayers in which blessings are said at various times of the day. The prayer to be said while washing one's hands before eating a meal or upon awakening in the morning is, "Blessed are You, Lord God, King of the Universe, who has sanctified us through your commandments and commanded us concerning the washing of hands." Therefore, every meal becomes a sacred ritual, requiring the prayerful washing of one's hands. Such daily rituals help one to see that all life is holy. The life of the traditional family is also shaped by a number of ritual duties. One of the most important is daily bathing, a ritual of cleansing spiritually and physically before prayer. Similarly, in a Catholic Mass the priest says the following prayer as he washes his hands at the time of offering the gifts of bread and wine: "Lord, wash away my iniquity; cleanse me from sin...." But these priestly prayers have rarely found their way into the bathrooms of rectories or the bathrooms or lives of those who attend Mass. Thich Nhat Hanh, the Buddhist monk and author, writes of the prayer of a Zen master, Doc The: "Washing my hands, I hope that every person will have pure hands to receive reality." And so we find rituals for the washing of hands in many great religious traditions. Our hands represent the whole person. By such prayers, we are rededicated to the Way and to God.

Perhaps we could all compose a personal prayer for washing our hands to remind ourselves that we are pilgrims of the Way. The following is a suggestion: "In washing my hands, I hope that all I do will be pure, clean of selfishness." Notice that the prayer begins with what is happening – washing hands. If we want to make the daily and ordinary activities of our lives prayerful and holy, we must first be aware of what we are do-

69

ing. Think about it. Do we not bring very little attention or mindfulness to brushing our teeth or moving our bowels? Instead of the mind being full of the present activity, we are busy with such so-called "important" things as solving problems, planning our day or replaying an old tape of some unpleasant personal exchange. We need to be reminded frequently that God can be found *only* in the present moment. We need to bring our wandering minds back to living in the present, regardless of how dull or trivial the activity seems. Such efforts to overcome "forgetfulness" are essential to anyone wanting to live a contemplative and mystical life. Taking a bath, combing one's hair or looking in a mirror all can be part of a continuous communion with the Divine Presence.

Each time we look into the bathroom mirror, we should remember that it is a magic mirror which can help us on the Way. Looking in the bathroom mirror is a good time to talk to ourselves. We are alone, and so there is no fear of being accused of vanity in taking extra time to look at ourselves. Looking at our image, we can speak words of encouragement or correction: "You drank too much last night, George...look at your eyes!" We can also examine the face in front of us with the eye of an inspector, noticing each new sign of aging. The bathroom with its private, magic mirror is a wonderful place for a mini-wake, a place to mourn our own deaths. If we can, as we pass through life, properly mourn our little deaths as each one comes — each new gray hair, new wrinkle or blemish — then we will die happy deaths. Proper mourning allows us to accept and embrace the aging process as natural. Those who pretend that they are not aging — dying slowly — who use creams, ointments and dyes to pretend it is otherwise, only find themselves in an impossible race with Old Boney Death.

Saint Jerome said, "The face is the mirror of the

70

mind, and eyes without speaking confess the secrets of the heart." As we daily examine our faces in the bathroom mirror we can dedicate ourselves to making the Divine Mystery the secret of our hearts. That Secret never ages and is eternally youthful. Each trip to the bathroom can be as sacred as the trip of Moses to Mt. Sinai.

With Edmund Wilson, Archimedes, Thoreau and many a poet and king, we agree that the bathroom is a place of inspiration, of ritual, of awakening, of death and dying, of prayer and play. From trimming our toenails to moving our bowels, we can rejoice that NOTHING is separated from our living communion with God. This reflection on the bathroom began with a quotation from a Vietnamese folk song, "Hardest of all is to practice the Way at home, second in the crowd, and third in the pagoda." Let us conclude with a line of a new folk song, "The *best* place to pray and follow the Way is at home."

# A Sexual Spirituality

Our contemporary society is the result of several revolutions. Some have been political, some technological and others cultural. But one that has influenced all of us is the sexual revolution that swept the Western World after the middle of this century. As a result of that revolution, sex was viewed much more freely and without guilt. Sex was no longer unspeakable and awful, but unfortunately it was no longer awe-full — surrounded by mystery and wonder. For the spiritual pilgrim, all life is wrapped in the awe, wonder and grandeur of the Divine Mystery. That halo of the holy also should surround our sexuality. So, much has been lost in the process; yet, this revolution was necessary. Because of an anti-sexual, anti-female theology, Christianity lacked a wholesome sexual spirituality. Sanctity was thought to be fully attained only by those who had renounced sexual desires and "risen above" the passions of the flesh.

This discrimination against sexual pleasures did not come from a biblical source but from the influence of certain Greek philosophy upon the early Church. Stoic philosophers sought the Absolute or Divine by renouncing the body, society, friendship and love. This attitude was reflected in the theology of men like St. Augustine, who lived in the mid-fourth century and set the course for many of our attitudes and moral judgments toward sexuality. St. Augustine and others considered it at least a venial sin even when the sexual act was performed by a husband and wife, primarily because it was viewed

as an act in which the participants were "out of control." However, Hebrew spirituality, from which the spirituality of Jesus came, viewed sex as a life-giving, healing continuation of the artistic creation of God. Although the Jewish society of our Lord's day, like many primitive societies, surrounded sexuality with certain taboos, they were set into place not because it was thought to be evil or vile, but to insure that it was considered awesome and powerful.

As citizens of a society that has made sexuality open and free, we must guard that, in our new-found freedom, we do not lose the sense of wonder and awe that is essential to this vital part of all human lives.

We need a more inclusive spirituality, a new way to interlock our sexuality with our search for the Divine Mystery. Such a spirituality must begin with the echo of God's exclamation of delight at the end of each day of creation — "That's GOOD!" We need to see all of creation with the eyes of our Creator-God, viewing everything of the earth, including our bodies, as an outpouring of the Divine Artist. Sexuality then, like speech, is a God-gift which has been given as a means for us to come to wholeness. To live without our gift of speech would be possible and might even help develop other gifts of God, but it would be a very unusual act of loving. The denial of the use of sexuality as an act of love for God has been traditionally viewed as exceptional, a special and rare gift of the Spirit. However, sexuality, the gift of the Spirit for the vast majority, has its own special charism, its own spiritual "secret mission."

The exploration of the erotic, like all great adventures, holds certain dangers. Our sexual energies hold great potency, and that very power can lead us away from the Mystery as well as into it. Perhaps it is the great danger surrounding this powerful need that caused earlier spiritual teachers to take the safer course and counsel a denial of it. But when adventure dies, so does

74

religion and life itself. And adventure plays on the edge of peril; it is the rich mixture of danger and the promise of fulfillment. One of the dangers of the adventure of human love is that while it is intended to liberate us from the ego, it holds the power to trap us even more deeply in the self and its needs.

Sexuality is wrapped in the sacred; it opens the door to ecstasy — to the very "loss of control" that so worried early theologians. By means of sexual love we can be taken "out of ourselves" — our little individualistic selves — and fused into our greater selves. We need only recall the marvelous story of creation and the Garden of Eden. God creates one person who appears to be androgynous, or at least self-contained. Then the Great Gardener divides the first human and makes Eve from his flesh. What was one is now two, and God calls them into oneness again as he says, "Become one — one flesh, one body!" Solid spirituality is always a return to that primal state of unity. Sexual instinct is, then, essentially a desire to come home, to restore once again that primal order, that original state of absolute unity and affectionate companionship with God. That order of the Garden existed before life became divided by sexual differences, which then unfolded in a seemingly endless series of differences: color, creed, nationality, political beliefs, the multiple divisions of humankind. And so, the sexual-spiritual quest brings all the fullness and richness of the diversity of creation into the primal union. Each person — married, single or vowed religious — who seeks the razor's edge that is called the Way, is involved in a sexual spirituality.

While we have made great progress in the movement from a sense of guilt about sexual desire and longing for union with another, we may not have come far enough! We need to move beyond biological knowledge, beyond certain religious attitudes that sex is "permitted" under certain social conditions, to a sense

75

that it can be a sacred act of worship. We need to approach our sexual love as a continuation of that original, divinely creative work. Creation is a continuous act, and when we live out the fullness of our sexuality, we become co-creators with God. It is also an act of redemption by which we are healed and made whole once again. And it provides a pattern for every deed and thought on the search for unity.

That quest involves three levels of intimacy. On the first level we seek, in the mystery of love and friend-

ship, to experience a communion of companionship. We enjoy the bodily presence of another whether that presence is erotic or not. There is intimacy in sharing the same office, home or fishing boat. Such a physical intimacy repels loneliness and holds the magic of healing. As friendship deepens and the intimacy begins to include the sharing of dreams and ideals, tales of defeat and victory, fears and doubts and petty feelings expressed without shame,we sense a liberation of spirit. To share with another and to know that this gift of self is treated with reverence and love is to know God, and to taste the delights of Eden. This intimacy of heart and sharing of soul is the second level of our return, of our reunion. The divided self is united by finding communion in love for the other. These first two levels are sexual without being genital. They possess a sacred power, allowing depths of intimacy that genital sexuality alone cannot give.

The third level of our spiraling return is found in the creative art of making love. This physical union, however, finds its ultimate pleasure and fulfillment when it is accompanied by a daily living out of the first two forms of intimacy. Bodily intimacy alone is hollow and incomplete, for it lacks the involvement of the whole person, making it a shallow shadow of total love. We find the ritual reflection of this primal sacrament of unity in the Christian tradition of the Eucharist. The Last Supper embodies the conditions by which love-making becomes ecstatic and creative. At that sacred supper Jesus says, "This is my body...given in love for you." Each time that we love, giving the gifts of body, blood, spirit, life – the all of who we are – we are taken beyond our limited selves and returned again to the Mystery from which all life has come. James Carroll once said, "Ninety-nine percent of all people are intended to pray in bed!" And their prayer is that of Christ at the Last Supper: "This is my body, this is my

blood, given in love." That level of consciousness makes the act of sexual lovemaking a sacred ritual of unity. It is no accident that it was seen by the first disciples of Jesus as a sacred sign of the Mystery of Christ and the Kingdom. St. Paul's epistle to the Ephesians proclaims it with poetic beauty: "So ought men to love their wives as their own bodies. He that loves his wife loves himself...for we are members of Christ's body, of his flesh, and of his bones.... This is a great mystery; but I speak concerning Christ and the Church" (Eph. 5:28-32). When our sexuality is viewed from this position, then it becomes truly "awe-full" and filled with wonder.

For those who, in earlier times, sexuality was not divided from life, it was in itself a symbol of life and fertility. How easy it is for us, as citizens of a technological age, to forget the need for fertility. We who obtain our food in packages from stores have become uprooted from the earth and growing things, from animals and their natural lives. But fertility and life are twins, and both require love, passion and creativity. All love, regardless of whether or not it takes on a physical expression, is intended to be creative; as Matthew Fox says it so well, "One plus one equals three." When love for another ceases to be fertile, to give birth to joy, service, beauty, harmony and compassion, we should examine it at once, for it is sick.

A symbol of the medical profession is the serpent. It also was regarded by the ancients as a sign of sexuality and, in the wider context, of fertility and healing. Intimacy at each of its three levels, but most of all at the third, has the power to cure the minor discords, the nicks and scratches of daily life. Its power to heal comes from the gift of unity that draws the lovers beyond themselves, coaxes them out of the petty prisons built by their own egos.

But if our love is to be fertile, creative, healing and

worshipful, we must provide the proper environment of leisure and humor. Pious persons may be shocked, but sex should happen more than once or twice a week; rather, it must be a constant activity. The giving of themselves in expressions of affection, service and kindness is the ceaseless love-making of all true lovers. Such passionate abandonment finds expression in doing the laundry, wiping dishes, listening to each other, being as intimate as possible at all times. All such simple acts of love are creative and liberating.

Professor Heiko Oberman of the University of Tubingen in West Germany speaks of how Luther, a former Augustinian friar who married, found the art of lovemaking not only delightful but sacred. In a letter to a friend, Luther is quoted as saying, "As you penetrate your wife, I'll penetrate mine, and we'll be united in Christ." Luther goes on to state that the best place to be at Christ's Second Coming is to be united in the act of making love. Such bold statements by a great religious genius support the spirituality that this chapter has proposed.

We who live in the desert of a secular and humanistic society, who have "gotten even" with God for throwing Adam and Eve out of the Garden by throwing God out of our twentieth century garden, must begin to shape a new spirituality of sexuality. These reflections are a simple and incomplete beginning. With trust in our capacity to hear with the inner ear — the ear of the heart — we can find our own spirituality in regard to love and sexuality, once we have moved beyond our old religious prejudices and our contemporary lack of awe. We must trust our inner voices even when they assert that there is goodness and beauty in what past ages have called evil and dirty. We need to trust our own sense of the sacred so that we can affirm that Presence particularly in the midst of experiences that are filled with life, passion and

pleasure.

And with that sense of trust in ourselves, especially in the human gifts of sex that God has given and in its primal call to unity, we need to add that all relationships that are fruitful and fun-filled require as much attention and creativity as we invest in our professions. Friendship and love are art forms and as such will not flourish without great care. But the rewards are the highest joys known to humans, for they are appetizers of the Absolute, a foretaste of heaven.

Finally, with the intimacy that flows from friendship comes the desire that it will never cease. Only intimacy can give birth to commitment, and when intimacy dies so does commitment. And when human intimacy dies, the spiritual quest also stalls out, becoming only a half-alive performance of religious duties. Only a passion for union can fuel our quest for the Divine Mystery. Every human carries the fundamental pain of separation and alienation which requires the touch of both human and divine love to be relieved. The wisdom-filled words of our Creator-God in the Garden contained rich implications for all seeking a secular sanctity in this age: "It is not good for one to be alone."

# Basic Disarmament
# and World Peace

The spirituality of the end of the twentieth century, a secular sanctity, must by necessity include the task of being a peacemaker. Living such a vocation is truly to become a "light of the world," which is to embrace that luminous possibility dreamed by Christ. His vision of holiness included the ability to love one's enemies and to seek good for them as well as for oneself. One wonders when such radical thoughts came to Jesus. Were they the fruit of his deep and intimate prayer life? Did they flow forth from those numerous times of silent withdrawal from the busyness of daily life? Indeed, Jesus himself tells us that his words are not his own but rather are those of his Father. If so, when did these sacred messages come to him, messages that are, even today, revolutionary in their call to loving non-violence as a way of life?

The Gospel of non-violence, love and peacemaking may have come to Jesus when he was involved in an activity we might find difficult even to imagine Jesus performing. Try to picture in your mind the image of Jesus trimming his fingernails or clipping his toenails! Yes, perhaps it was during this most human and routine act of bodily care that the message of compassion and non-violence so characteristic of Jesus' teachings may have come to him.

Jesus trimming his fingernails? I realize that we would hardly look upon this weekly chore as a time of transcendental enlightenment — it's an activity to which we rarely give a second thought. Yet, to those

83

of previous ages this human chore was far from insignificant. The prophet Mohammed listed it among the qualities of a prophet, saying: "...clipping the mustache, not cutting or shaving the beard; cleansing the teeth and cutting the nails...." Now while we dismiss both the chore and our nail and hair clippings themselves as unimportant, the ancients did not. Sir James Frazer in his book *Taboo and Perils of the Soul* tells how certain primitive peoples took great care of what they did with their clippings of hair and nails. Some feared that birds would come and pick them up and build nests with them. And if this happened, it would cause the head to ache. (The next time you have a headache, as you reach for an aspirin, you might ask yourself, "What did I do with my fingernail clippings?") The people of Carpathia believed that if mice carried off the clippings it would cause idiocy, and those of Southern India buried their clippings to prevent harm. There is an old expression, dating back to Petronius: "Cut neither nails nor hair at sea." It seems that the cuttings of one's nails or hair were votive offerings made to the Greek goddess Persephone. Beware, then, of making such offerings at sea, in the kingdom of the sea god Neptune. Such holy gifts to another god would only arouse his jealousy — and who knows what might happen to your ship? But the point is that those clippings we so easily dispose of were actually sacred gifts to the gods and goddesses. Among certain Moslem sects, the clippings are kept safely in a handkerchief to be buried along with the person at the time of death. It is a bit of innocent trivia that among certain Moslems there is a custom of breaking each hair clipping so as to release the guardian angel within it.

And you — what do you do with your nail clippings? I must confess that I have been tempted to leave mine scattered carelessly about so that mice might use them to build their nests. Then I would have a good

84

excuse for my occasional outbreaks of lunacy or lapses in logic! Perhaps, at this moment, you are saying to yourself, "A chapter about trimming fingernails? I think the mice have already made a nest of his fingernail clippings." But, before you skip this chapter, be patient and read on a bit more. All this care and concern was given to fingernail and hair clippings by those in ages long past because they were thought to have profound meaning. For mice or birds to carry them off was to lose an essential part of themselves. Out of fairness to the wisdom of the past, please reflect for a while on your fingers and their nails.

Your fingernails and toenails are composed of hardened skin cells. It is the very same material that also makes up the claws of animals and birds! Are, then, your fingernails a relic of pre-human instruments of attack? Are those well-manicured nails also the last vestiges of humanity's oldest weapons – the hands? And consider the arrow, the first manufactured missile – isn't it simply an extension of the finger with its sharpened, pointed nail? If so, then each time you trim your fingernails, you are involved in primitive arms-limitation, in the earliest and most basic of all disarmament.

King David, saint, singer, poet and warrior of Israel, with insight, says in verse 1 of Psalm 144, "Blessed be the Lord, my rock, who trains my fingers for war." Our hands are the primal weapons, and we have faint memories of their former use as instruments of anger. Today, in moments of anger, we unconsciously shake a finger at someone, or in another form of attack – accusation – we point a finger. We know that anxious persons sometimes chew their nails. It may be that they are biting back the urge to attack, to resolve their frustration and anxiety by violence. And perhaps as Jesus trimmed his fingernails, he may have reflected on humanity's inclination to use them as weapons. And

85

as he did, perhaps he heard, deep within his heart, the voice of God calling him to total disarmament.

Each time that he trimmed his nails, perhaps he became aware that within him was a dark and dangerous power, always present and always in need of trimming. That "dark power" is never fully removed any more than our fingernails are clipped and filed down once and for all. If we wish to be peacemakers, we must be involved in a continuous and loving act of self-disarmament and internal peacemaking. From the middle of this century onward, the issue of arms control, disarmament, and the need of nuclear military abstinence has grown to critical importance. Christ's radical challenges to non-violence now appear not simply as poetic but rather as indispensible. President Dwight Eisenhower once said, "I think that people want peace so much that one of these days government had better get out of their way and let them have it." But is that true? Do we really want peace? The concern of peace is more than an election issue; it is now a moral one. And as such it confronts the morality of all good and decent people. "Good and decent people" – that's us, isn't it? And the warmongers – well, they're the world leaders, the generals and military leaders at whom we can point or shake a finger, demanding that they do something.

Such self-righteousness is only the denial of the dark shadow within each of us. That shadow is inseparable from our human psyches, a fact that Jesus knew and understood well. The urge to deny the darkness – to be self-righteous – is a powerful one for each of us. Early in childhood we begin to cast our dark shadows onto others, blaming them for what is wrong while we present ourselves as blameless. Our primal parents, Adam and Eve, are the classic objects of such projections. So, who are the warmongers – the Russians, the Iranians? Yes, but so are we! Each one

86

of us possesses and uses violence in countless and cleverly camouflaged ways. Carl Jung says, "Everyone carries a shadow, and the less it is embodied in the individual's conscious life, the blacker and denser it is."

The earth will be rid of war only when each of us humbly admits to the presence of the dark shadow

within. Only when we acknowledge the hidden desire for aggression and division – the death instinct – can the world move toward peace. That movement toward total disarmament occurs at the pace with which you and I dis-arm ourselves of the weapons of domination and control. The question is not so much, "When will

the nations of the world disarm?" but "When will you and I disarm?"

Indeed, Jesus reminded us of God's commandment, "You shall not kill." But he adds, "I say to you that you cannot even be angry with another without being guilty of murder!" The call, then, is to a higher consciousness. More than a negative commandment, it calls us to love our enemies. This is, of course, the most radical of all disarmament — to free ourselves of angry, harmful thoughts. To disarm the missiles of our minds is truly total disarmament. Those seeking Christ-consciousness acknowledge that within them is the full measure of evil — and also of good. And only in the loving interaction of the darkness and the light, of these seemingly opposite powers, does the divinely human appear.

True meekness can only come from such a marriage of darkness and light, a living companionship of the two. For only when we are consciously able to acknowledge and embrace the abiding presence of the darkness within can we become "the light of the world." Only then can we let our lights shine forth to give glory to God. Each time we trim back our primal weapons, our nails, we can remind ourselves to be conscious of the inner presence of the instincts of aggression and division.

The bathroom, as has been considered before, is an excellent shrine and place of prayer. Since it is the normal place for the routine of nail clipping, it might be the place to make that routine into a holy ritual. A brief prayer such as this might aid that ritual of nail clipping:

Lord, as I trim my fingernails
may I transform my inner aggression into love.
May I, by your grace, seek in every way
to live as a peacemaker.

Each time I trim my nails, I shorten my claws and physically disarm myself. I do so with the knowledge that my fingernails, like the darkness within me, can be used for both good or bad purposes. With properly trimmed nails I can pick up a pin or thread a needle, turn a page or open an envelope. And if I am a guitar player, I can trim the nails of my fingers to form picks with which to make beautiful music.

Peace comes not only when we beat our swords into plowshares but also when we trim our fingernails into instruments of music, turning hostility into harmony, chaos into chorus and domination into dance. Those who do so have lovingly embraced the twin powers of darkness and light within, acknowledging that they can embrace their "enemies" as well. Only then is it possible to understand the challenge of Christ, "When your enemy strikes you on one cheek, offer him the other." At surface hearing, such a command appears to be pure madness, as an invitation to more pain and shame. But reflect a moment: why did Christ call us to offer the other cheek rather than to do nothing at all?

To "turn the other cheek" is not just a passive acceptance but rather a positive hope that instead of another blow the person will be called by our loving non-violence to an act of love. Instead of a blow on the cheek they are invited to kiss it! Remember that in the Near East, the ritual kiss of greeting is given on *both* cheeks. To turn the other cheek is first an act of profound hope and secondly an expression of faith in the evolutionary nature of every human. As an act of faith it proclaims that there exists in the enemy a full measure of compassion seeking to express itself. Only those who have seen and lovingly embraced both the goodness and evil within themselves can believe that these twins also reside in even the worst of humanity. Those who wish to be "the light of the world" must be supreme optimists who believe that love has the power

89

to bring alive in others the divinely human potential.

In the ugly face of the ultimate terror of nuclear war and the destruction of the planet, what do we do? We vote, we work for disarmament of nations, we support arms control and we acknowledge that we have options other than war. We acknowledge that there are ways of resolving the problems of the human family other than by violence and military escalation. All this is needed, but it is much more necessary that each of us disarm ourselves.

As often as our nails need trimming, so do our minds need to shed the perennial weapons of self-defense — the words and deeds of sarcasm, superiority and ridicule. Let us turn this weekly task into a quiet reflection on personal and global disarmament.

# 21st Century Prophets

As we prepare for the year 2000, which is only a few years away, we will find an increasing interest by people in a spiritual activity that might be called prophecy-prayer. The ancient prophet of Israel, Joel, who lived about 2,400 years ago, spoke of a global vocation to prophecy when he said, "Your sons and daughters shall prophesy, your old shall dream dreams, your young shall see visions, and I will pour out my spirit upon all humanity." This vision of the prophet Joel is of a future time when the entire human family is prophetic, instead of a special person or class of people. In our spiritual history the function of the prophet has been to receive the word of God, speak it to the people, and so affirm the basic beliefs and the relation between God and ourselves. Joel's vision of a universal Pentecost was but an expansion of the wish of the great prophet Moses, who said, "I wish that all the Lord's people were prophets and that the Lord would confer his Spirit upon them all!" That wish of Moses and the vision of Joel speak to a personal need of each of us today in these last hours of the twentieth century. Has that global downpour of the Spirit already happened – not upon a special person or priestly caste but rather upon all the human family – or are we still waiting for such a cosmic cloudburst?

We associate the future with prophets and seers. Tomorrow, it seems, is the time frame in which they have the greatest interest. We all are concerned about that point of time – the future, whether it be next week

or the next century. Tomorrow and all the tomorrows after it are of great importance to us, or we would not spend so much energy and money preparing for that future. After the rapid changes of the past fifteen years, we are anxious about what the next fifteen may bring us. The owner of the small gas station is concerned about the location of a proposed interstate highway. The farmer is concerned about the price of wheat next year, and the worker wonders if he will have enough retirement money to live in comfort. All of us have an interest in the future. That interest can be about the next century or the next weekend. We watch the long-range forecast of the weather on the evening news with interest, or scan astrological charts in the newspaper. These are modern media prophets who appeal to our primal human desire to know about the future. That interest is growing, and book sales reveal our concern. In 1945, only thirty-five science fiction novels were published (science fiction being the literature that deals with life in the future), but in 1975 there were 900 such novels printed. That number would be much higher for this year. We are a people in search of what is ahead of us and what we can expect from the future. Preparing for the future is a survival need. In his book *Future Shock* Alvin Toffler observed, "Under conditions of high-speed change, a democracy (and here instead of 'democracy' you can insert your own name or the words family, church or community) without the ability to anticipate condemns itself to death!"

Anticipation is that ability to look forward and to predict an action in advance. To anticipate in that sense is the work of the religious prophet. Is such a power of anticipation the promised global downpour of the Spirit? With such a gift, humanity would not need fortune tellers, psychics or prophets to help them anticipate the future, for everyone would know how to practice that science.

94

In our modern society, our prophets are usually not professionally religious persons and are frequently considered to be agnostic. They are usually found not in temples but in the arts. They are also found in the ranks of the mentally ill. Poets, writers, artists and moviemakers attempt to help us anticipate the future by showing a vision of it today. Orwell's book *1984* revealed a world in which ordinary people had little or no control of their lives. It was a mythical statement about what is happening today in numerous ways, but it was written many years ago. Jules Verne and Buck Rogers were also prophets. The motion picture *A Clockwork Orange* shocked audiences with its senseless violence, which only a few years later was commonplace evening news. The prophetic statements of such artists usually go unheard, and we can wonder about the reason for our inability to respond to their warnings.

Patients in our mental hospitals and in the waiting rooms of psychologists also predict the future. These persons do so by living out consciously what the rest of us are able to keep unconscious; that is, at least for today! The psychosomatically sick members of our society, for certain reasons, have less resistance to the approaching emotional stresses of daily life and so fall victim to those stresses. The patients are predicting in their personal struggles the affliction that will eventually break out on all sides in our society. The mentally ill are the prophets of tomorrow—as are poets, painters and film makers—for they also tell us what to anticipate. The present common anxiety about the future and about the meaning of life is a common possession of vast numbers of people that first appeared in mental patients in the late 1930's and early 1940's. We can wonder if the emotional problems of loneliness and self-isolation of today's mental patients will, in the year 2000, be household afflictions like the common cold.

Prophets, painters and mental patients should act

95

like social alarm clocks to awaken us to what is happening in order that we might change our life patterns and values. But the jangling alarm bell runs down, and we continue to live asleep, unable to see the future of our families, our marriages or religious communities. We close our ears and eyes to these prophetic alarms because we have the ability to blind ourselves to those aspects of life that we feel are beyond our control. We block out from our consciousness the continuous flow of prophecies because the Coming Apocalypse seems to be beyond our personal control. But the future of our marriages and families, or even our own personal futures, does not lie in the year 2000. That future is being created by us today, here and now, in the midst of our daily lives.

Contrary to common belief, it was the life of "today" that was of the most concern to the ancient religious prophets. Only if the people hardened their hearts today to the message of life would the ugly tomorrow of fire, smoke and destruction become a reality. The anxiety of our ever-changing age should awaken us to prayer, the prayer of the prophets — anticipation! We are also called to live out the anticipation of the prophets — prayer!

Prophetic prayer is the ability to see, not to foresee. It is simply to see today in a clear and realistic manner. If I do not wish to become a victim of tomorrow, in the words of *Future Shock*, "condemning myself to death," then I must learn to pause, taking time to look closely at my life and what is happening to me today. The prophet-playwright Eugene Ionesco in his play *The Bald Soprano* reveals the result of a failure to pause and look closely at life. In this play, a man and woman happen to meet and engage in polite conversation. As they visit, they discover that they both came down to New York from New Haven that morning on the same 10 o'clock train. They also find that they are staying

96

at the same address on Fifth Avenue and that they both have a seven-year-old daughter. Suddenly they realize that they are man and wife! Ionesco's husband and wife did not suddenly become strangers to one another on that 10 o'clock train from New Haven. Their failure to anticipate the gradual separation between them is not unique. How many husbands and wives live lives that prevent them from truly knowing one another because of their excessive involvement in their children? How many religious, in the name of service, live lives that lead to making them strangers within their own communities? Such isolation is the result of a failure to anticipate what life will be like when the children are grown and gone or what life will be like when we are retired and unable to lose ourselves in work. We are all intended to be prophets, persons extremely concerned about the quality of life today. Such persons know that tomorrow is but the total of a thousand todays. If today my life is unhappy, without meaning or purpose, why will tomorrow be anything other than a monstrous emptiness?

Unless I am able to take time this day to pause and look at my life, I shall not be able to anticipate the future. The name of that pause for anticipation is prayer. "If you invoke me and pray to me, I will listen to you; when you seek me, you shall find me; if you search with all your heart, I will let you find me, says the Lord" (Jer. 29:13-14). The prayer of the prophet, then, is not some crystal ball with which to see the future, but rather the ability to see more clearly the present. Seek the present, which is life, with all your heart and do so with the confidence of being gifted with the fullness of life. As prophetic people, the task is not to foresee the tomorrows of 2001, but to enable that tomorrow to come into being. We are creating the year 2001 by enabling the sort of life and relationships we wish to experience at that future time — enabling them

to come into existence by work and effort in the midst of our today.

Those persons who can take (or is that "steal"?) time daily to see their lives and relationships clearly will find happiness in the future. We have a certain fascination with fortune-tellers and with psychic predictors. What we need is the same fascination with the condition and quality of today. The future looms beneath the horizon with horrible predictions of over-population, of the earth-melting heat of nuclear toys, of the ozone-eating SST's and of our lives controlled by the government with its police force of computers. Personally, we wonder and fearfully consider our own apocalypse. Perhaps this could be in a nursing home staring at a blank wall with mind and body heavily tranquilized, or struggling to survive on a limited income while paying $150 for a pair of shoes we could have purchased in 1984 for only $35, or wondering if we will be alone, without anyone to love us and care for us as we sit behind our triple-locked door and barred windows seeking safety from the violence and terrorism of society. Whatever the future, Jesus continuously told us not to worry about tomorrow. "So do not be anxious about tomorrow; tomorrow will look after itself" (Matt. 6:34). Yes, tomorrow will look after itself if we look after today.

That attitude toward the future requires a good deal of faith and prayer. First, we need the faith to believe that our tomorrows are indeed made from the "stuff" of today. Secondly, we need the practice of prayer which gives the ability to see clearly what is the "stuff" of which our todays are constructed. Are we really too busy to pray, to take time to be still, or do we keep busy so as *not* to look at the "stuff" of our todays? If tomorrow is to be for us a promised land, we will need faith, prayer and a spirit of spontaneity that will allow us to move freely with whatever is happening. In

98

Japanese poetry there is a form called Haiku which is a brief three-line poem. The ancient master, Kohyo, expressed in three lines what all these words have attempted to say:

> The dragonfly
> Perches on the stick
> Raised to strike him.

The dragonfly, like the prophet, is super-alert. The dragonfly has realized the situation with keen insight. How can the person with the fly swatter kill the dragonfly if it is sitting on the fly swatter? The dragonfly is preserving its life by acting spontaneously. We need to sit in such alertness, which is the basic condition for prophetic prayer. We must, as Jesus said, "watch and pray." Is peace and an experience of the fullness of God a future quality of life for which we are willing to set aside ten minutes each day for stillness and quiet prayer? Ten minutes a day is so little time out of so many hours to sit like a dragonfly on the fly swatter — still, quiet and watching.

We cannot prepare for the future by stocks and bonds, or by insurance policies or ironclad securities, but only by learning to live today, fully alive and alert. Retirement plans and bank accounts can only assist us to survive, but sitting like Kohyo's dragonfly can show us truly how to live now and in the future.

# Suggestions on Dragonfly Sitting

When a dragonfly sits, it sits. Its attention is focussed on the act of perching on the end of a stick — not upon its future flights, its past adventures or some exciting or unpleasant encounter with another dragonfly. My point is that, unlike humans, a dragonfly simply sits.

The silent prayer of meditation is not a reflection upon an event or person, even a holy one. Meditation, as a form of contemplative prayer, is what sitting is to a dragonfly. Unfortunately our minds do not lend themselves to living so totally in the present moment; they are constantly busy elsewhere. When we "sit" we become uncomfortably aware of this "hopping about" of the mind.

If we wish to sit quietly absorbed in the present moment — in the presence of the Divine Mystery who dwells only in this sacred moment — we must first learn to sit still. We begin to still our restless bodies (for which doing nothing is a cause for much distress) by sitting

on floor or chair with our backs as straight as possible without strain and with hands in a comfortable position. We quiet the body further by gently observing our breathing. Making the breath smooth and quiet harmonizes the body, tuning it like a harp. Once we have "tuned" the body, we then begin to quiet the mind by gently discarding all but the present moment.

While there are many excellent methods to still the mind, I will only mention one. It involves the repetition of a sacred word, such as one of the beautiful names of God or a single word such as love, peace or a sacred word from another language. We begin to recite this word inwardly, allowing the conscious mind to be absorbed simply in the sound of the word and not in its meaning. This combination of silent speaking and listening to the word is to be done with gentleness and never with force.

The first rule of meditation is *no work*, in the sense that we do not strain to focus our attention; instead, we relax and allow the prayer-word to carry us inward to the temple of the heart. Nor do we work to drive away the unending parade of thoughts that longs to crowd out our absorption in the prayer-word. When we become aware that an alien thought is intruding, we gently turn our attention back, with loving devotion, to our prayer-word.

It will not be easy for the "self" to dissociate itself from its thoughts and emotions in this return to the prayer-word. We will want to judge our meditation as "good" or "bad" by our ability to control these thoughts. And this brings us to the second rule of meditation: *no judging*. We should never judge our prayer as good or bad, even if we have had to return to our prayer-word a thousand times in one fifteen- or twenty-minute sitting. The only bad meditation is not meditating at all! Every attempt to sit with devotion and zeal is a good meditation.

101

The third rule is *no profit!* For busy, "productive" people this is one of the most difficult. We want to see results from our efforts. We don't want to waste our time. Yet prayer is always a waste of time when viewed from the point of profit. We enter into prayer, especially the contemplative prayer of meditation, as an act of love. We give a gift of our time to God for all the gifts that we have received. What more precious gift than time do we have to give? We come, then, to these twenty minutes seeking nothing: no mystical states, no spiritual powers nor even the gift of inner peace. Even "holy" thoughts should not be listened to when we repeat the prayer-word. Our minds are amazingly clever and use every trick possible to tempt us to return to thinking. We must come only to sit and open ourselves to the silent music of the mystery we call God. We come day after day, with self-discipline and with devotion, aware that the fruit of meditation is not to be sought in our meditation!

The fruit of meditation reveals itself in our daily lives, after we have finished our sitting. Slowly we begin to perceive a transformation in our behavior. With the passage of time – days, months, years – we begin to find a sense of balance in the movements of our emotions. That balance is called peace. With the passage of time we begin to sense a communion with all nature, with others and with God. But we do not meditate even for these reasons. We enter it freely, seeking nothing but to sit still in the love of God as we use the prayer-word to quiet our minds.

Finally, we are by nature a people of ritual. So we may find it helpful to enclose our fifteen or twenty minutes of meditation (dragonfly sitting) within a frame of other prayer forms. We aid our prayer discipline by choosing the same time (before rather than after meals) and the same place each day. The use of a special corner and a prayer rug is helpful; so is the creation of

a small shrine area. Incense and a candle can further increase the sense of worship and ritual. But whatever the form, it is important that our personal silent prayers are expressions of our own needs. We may wish to experiment with these and other external aids to meditation. But the one thing we should not change is our sacred prayer-word. We should remain faithful to the word which seems correct and meaningful. The usual temptation is to judge (a violation of the second rule) that there is no progress and that changing words will help. We must resist this temptation unless we feel strongly, for reasons that flow from grace and prayer, that the word should be changed. Also, when we arrive at a method, we should stay with it until it becomes an organic part of us before seeking — if ever — something new. Those who are fortunate will have a spiritual director to lead them; but everyone has access to the greatest of all spiritual guides, our Lord.

Meditation is the most simple prayer. It calls for no special talent. It only asks for a small investment of time — fifteen minutes morning and evening, or at least once a day. The reason we fail to harvest the fruits of the prayer of sitting is that we lack the self-discipline to surrender even that small particle of time to God each day. But if we can learn, with patience and persistence, to set aside that little time to travel inward, we will find that the voice of *the* Guide will lead us where we need to go. Once we have set our feet on the pathway of the spiritual quest and follow it with a holy passion, all we need, when we need it, will come. We need only to be awake and open to the movement of God in our hearts — sitting still like our friend the dragonfly — to claim the infinite treasure, to be truly transformed.

# The Web-Communion
# of Saints

One of the first areas of modern culture to break with the strongly religious world of the Middle Ages was that of science. The scientific method intended to base on observation and experimentation what previously had been accepted on faith. However, it is interesting to note that modern science is making discoveries that are profound in their religious implications.

The discovery of the sacred in the midst of the secular scientific world is no more clearly seen than in the theories of an English plant physiologist, Rupert Sheldrake. Sheldrake has startled the scientific world with his theories of genetic learning. He sees nature not controlled by laws but by "habits." These habits are resonating fields of energy (morphogenetic or M-fields) that affect the development of life, from tiny crystals to our behavior as humans. Sheldrake offers several examples of his hypothesis. One concerns the work of Harvard professor William McDougall who taught rats to run a difficult water maze and found that each new generation of rats learned the maze more easily. This seemed to prove that some characteristics could be inherited. But when two other researchers attempted to duplicate McDougall's experiments, they discovered that their rats already knew the maze! Somehow the maze had now become a part of rat consciousness.

Another example, the "one hundredth monkey" theory, concerns the transfer of a large number of monkeys from their usual habitat to some islands in the Pacific Ocean. Their reaction to the new environ-

ment was being observed by scientists. The monkeys began to dig up yams found on the islands and eat them, dirt and all. One day a certain monkey on one of the islands took his yam to the ocean and washed it off before eating it. The next day two other monkeys did the same; each day others followed their actions until a "critical" number was reached. The scientists called this one the "one hundredth monkey." When the one hundredth monkey began to wash his yam, all the monkeys on the island began washing their yams before eating them. But the surprise was that all the monkeys on the other islands, separated geographically, began to wash their yams at the same time!

Sheldrake states that a field of energy acted as a communication system that gave the monkeys this evolutionary knowledge. This M-field, which exists outside of time and space, is like a blueprint of genetic knowledge operating at some subatomic level. What we call our "genetic structure" may then be a device for receiving messages from this resonating "broadcast field." This theory has vast implications because, if it is true, a great wealth of knowledge, ideas, creativity and wisdom would be available from those who have gone before us! This may sound like madness but before you put aside this book and turn on your television set, reflect on the words of a thirteenth century Islamic saint, Saadi of Shiraz. He said, "Pluck the cotton wool of heedlessness from the ear of awareness, so that the wisdom of dead men may reach your ear." This statement by a thirteenth century mystic could be what Sheldrake's M-field is all about!

If Saadi of Shiraz and Sheldrake are correct, then the source of learning is not simply the rational brain. Unlike monkeys and rats, perhaps, we humans need a special state of being to hear the signals broadcast by the M-field. Our normal waking state is one form of consciousness, and the twilight period of half-sleep

another. Sleep is a third and meditation creates a fourth state of consciousness. Each of these can be measured scientifically and has its own distinctive brain waves. When we are in the "beta" state (normal waking consciousness), we are unable to hear the signals of the M-field. But when we switch off that state and turn to another consciousness, we become receptive to this communication. The Old Testament contains a story about just such a possibility.

The youthful prophet Samuel, sleeping in the temple, near the ark, was awakened by a voice calling his name. So he went to his teacher who was nearby and asked if he had called him. The teacher said that he had not. Samuel went back to sleep and the experience was repeated a second and third time. His teacher finally explained that this was no earthly voice and told him to answer, "Speak, Lord, your servant is listening," if he should hear it again. When Samuel obeyed, he was visited by God. During his sleep Samuel had entered another state of consciousness. This does not mean that we should sleep in church. But if we wish to be all we might become and to receive directions for our personal mystic journeys, we might begin to be open to the morphogenetic field. If we are to hear with the inner ear, we will have to learn how to sit still. Buddha insightfully speaks of the same need when he says, "Seeker — meditate constantly. If you cannot quiet yourself, what will you ever learn? With a quiet mind come into that empty house, your heart, and feel the joy of the Way."

Stillness of body and mind in meditation is not easy, as anyone who daily attempts to quiet the whole person knows. Most of our waking hours are spent at the surface level of consciousness. When we pause and move from that level to a deeper one, an inner voice begins chanting, "Get up, go back to work, move around. There are more important things to do...." The demands of life and work require that we live most of

our day at the surface of our consciousness. However, it is counterproductive to wholeness and wellness to spend *all* of our waking hours in external awareness. We all need to take time to become inwardly quiet by learning to sit still.

Once a man went to visit a certain saintly man. When the visitor arrived he found the holy man in prayer. He sat so still that not even a hair of his head moved. When the holy man had finished his prayer, the visitor asked where he had learned such stillness. He replied, "From my cat. She was watching a mouse hole with even greater concentration than you have seen in me." The holy man's cat was seeking something with all her heart and soul. Such seeking gives power. The intensity of desire gives one the power to return, day after day, to the "hot-seat" of sitting still. If we are making little headway on our spiritual quest, perhaps we should ask ourselves if we are seeking our goal with the same passion that a cat seeks a mouse. And if we are seeking holiness-wholeness, we can rejoice because, if Rupert Sheldrake and a multitude of mystics in all ages and all religions are correct, we do not have to do it alone!

We do not have to begin our spiritual journeys from scratch; we can tap into the wisdom of saints and holy ones who have gone before us. As St. Saadi of Shiraz, the Moslem mystic, said, "Pluck the cotton wool of heedlessness from the inner ear" and learn the wisdom of the saints. When we discipline ourselves to sit still in prayer-meditation with the devotion of a cat intent upon a supper of mouse, we open ourselves to a special state of consciousness. In that state, those who have gone before us may be able to help us find creative solutions to our problems and guide us along the razor-sharp spiritual pathway. Sitting still and being quiet is a way to be "in tune." When a piano and a harp placed in the same room are tuned to the same pitch and a note is

108

struck on the piano, the same note sounds instantly on the harp! When we are "in tune," we respond as the harp echoes the note struck on the piano. Perhaps you have already thought of an older name hinted at for the morphogenetic field — that mysterious connection with those of the present and past. Could we not substitute for "M-field" the term we have known since childhood, the "Communion of Saints"?

That reality, the "Communion of Saints," is one of the mysteries of Christianity. The term is first found in the Apostle's Creed, a summation of Christian belief, which appeared around 150-200 A.D. The term means that all living people are united with all the holy dead and the saints in heaven. That unity also binds angelic spirits with all persons on earth who are in union with God by living good and holy lives. "Prayer is of all things of the spirit the one in which this communion or

109

fellowship is most active..." (Attwater's Catholic Dictionary). It has been our constant belief that this communion or divine web allows grace and energy to flow among all who are essential parts of the communion. Rupert Sheldrake maintains that in the M-field time and space are transcended; the same is true for the Communion of Saints. We rejoice in the communion, in the unity of love that is not destroyed by death. Many people have felt at one time or another the intercession of a friend, parent or child who has already passed through the doorway of death.

Charles Lindbergh in his book *The Spirit of Saint Louis* described an experience that sounds like the M-field-Communion of Saints. In the eighteenth hour of his flight across the Atlantic, he became tired and was having difficulties in his navigation when he began to experience himself as "an awareness spreading through space, over the earth and into the heavens, unhampered by time or substance." He felt that the fuselage of his tiny plane was filled with ghostly presences – "vaguely outlined forms, transparent, moving, riding weightless with me in the plane." He said that those presences conversed with him, advised him on problems of his navigation, "giving messages of importance, unattainable in ordinary life." Lindbergh stated that these "presences" seemed to be neither intruders nor strangers; it was more like a gathering of family and friends long separated. Many years after his historic flight, Lindbergh confessed that this mystical experience radically changed his life. He wrote, "Death no longer seems the final end it used to be but rather the entrance to a new and free existence." Or take the case of the great musician-genius, Wolfgang Mozart. When asked how he created such marvelous masterpieces of music he is said to have replied, "I only play the music I hear."

What is the source of Mozart's music and Lind-

bergh's messages? Perhaps we might also open ourselves to the cosmic web of all life − whatever we call it − and, plucking the cotton wool from our inner ears, listen for messages. The possibilities of such a sacred reality are almost unbelievable. We could be assisted by the wisdom of people like Picasso, Joan of Arc, Einstein, Francis of Assisi, Moses, Sarah, Buddha, Mozart, Mother Seton, Lao Tzu, Saadi of Shiraz and, of course, Jesus. Our friends and families who have become one with God could also assist us in this life-journey.

Perhaps prayer and meditation may be understood as a sort of seance. We are familiar with the gathering of persons who sit in the dark and await spiritual messages − taps and raps on the table which are said to come from the dead. While the word "seance" comes from the French and means "a sitting" and also from the Old French which means "to sit," there are important differences in the styles of sitting. In prayer we "sit still" not so much to receive messages, but to be in harmony and communion with the Divine Mystery. The first rule of good prayer is "no profit," because one enters into it not to "get something," but to give something − love, worship, adoration. One attends a seance for a practical purpose, and prayer as an act of love is without practical purposes. However, when we come to a time of prayerful communion and also present to God a difficulty for which we are seeking a solution, we may rise up from prayer with an insight to a problem. It is worth noting that before Jesus selected the twelve who were to be his apostles, he spent time in silence and prayer. St. Luke tells us, "Then he went out to the mountain to pray, spending the night in communion with God. At daybreak he called his disciples and selected twelve of them to be his apostles" (Lk. 6:12-13).

Prayer to God, in communion with the saints and

with prayerful devotion to them, may then be something much more than a relic of some superstitious age. Today, devotion to the saints does not seem present in our daily lives. But ask yourself a practical question. Ordinary people, common folk, are the most practical of people. Is it reasonable that devotion to the saints could have existed for centuries and centuries, unless those who practiced these prayerful devotions were experiencing something tangible in their prayer? Common folk, being very practical, would have dropped their devotion to the saints long ago – unless their prayers were being answered. What happened when people prayed to Saint Anthony to find their lost articles, or to Saint Blaise for health or to Saint Jude for some impossible solution? Theologically, it is true that the Divine Mystery is the source of all gifts and blessings, but does that exclude the mysterious influence of the Communion of Saints? Perhaps devotion to the saints has opened people to the possibility of assistance, and so a solution occurred. There is a saying, "The God you believe in is the God you experience." If you do not believe in something, does that cancel the reality? If we Christians really believe in the Communion of Saints – really pray the Apostle's Creed – should we not be as open to "messages" as Lindbergh or Mozart?

We need to let go of listening to only the rational, logical and practical side of our consciousness, and begin to listen to the feminine, intuitive and mystical side of our intelligence. None of us fully knows our personal place in the evolution (continuous creation) of human life. You could be the first (as was the first monkey who washed his yam) or you could be the critical hundredth person. First or last, each person is important to the completion of creation. Our personal efforts to achieve peace, inner harmony, social justice and reform are not isolated efforts, but form a united movement that lifts the human family upward to
112

greater spiritual heights. Our personal efforts to be faithful to prayer, to a time of sitting still, of meditation, are essential. In the East is the expression, "The Zen master sits (meditates) for the universe." Each time you "sit," your peace is for and in union with the universe. Each time you choose reconciliation instead of hostility, you make the possibility of peace a greater reality in the world. We will not, in all probability, see the New Age of peace and justice in our lifetime, but by our daily efforts to live whole and holy lives, we are passing on Christ-consciousness to those who are living now and to those who will come after us.

Let us conclude with a few lines recalled from George Bernard Shaw's play, *Saint Joan*. The play is about Joan of Arc, an uneducated, seventeen-year-old peasant girl in France. She lived in the middle of the fifteenth century, when the English occupied a part of France. In her prayer, Saint Joan heard voices that told her to place Charles VII on the French throne and to win back France from the English. Faithful to her prayer, the voices told her how to wage the war against the English. Historians call this illiterate seventeen-year-old girl a military genius! In Shaw's play the king, a weak man, is upset because he does not hear the voices. He says to Joan, "Why do I not hear your voices? Am I not the king? Should they not be speaking to me instead of to you, a simple peasant girl?" And Saint Joan answers, "My Leige, you too can hear them, but you must learn to listen. Listen after the trilling of the angelus bells. In the stillness, after the bells have ceased, listen, and then, my Leige, you too will hear the voices."

# ¿The Virtue of Questioning?

In response to a question of how to keep your youth, the author Ashley Montagu replied, "Well, the trick is very simple – to die young as late as possible!" Hidden within that simple yet profound reply is the art of preserving the spirit of a child. Within the spirit of the child are the expressions of humor, playfulness and curiosity. The last is the basic human desire to be an explorer. Since the Kingdom of which Jesus spoke is *life*, it is logical that he would say that only children might enter it – those who die young, at whatever age.

Christianity is filled with symbols. These visual signs that speak of the invisible include the cross, the dove, the boat, the egg, the lily, the anchor, the sun and many more. A new symbol for Christianity as a religion of youthfulness would be the question mark. As a new religious symbol, the question mark could be more powerful in our daily lives than the sign of the cross! As a punctuation mark the "?" resembles the "!" and both appear at the end of a line of words. The question mark, however, has bowed its head in humility and has asked a question instead of making a bold statement. Because the "?" approaches life with the spirit of an explorer, it is the sign of the child and it is a sacred sign. There are two ways to say the simple truth that God is love. We could say, "God is love!" Or we could say, "God is love?" The second way opens us up to an entire process of wonder and exploration. The child within would say, "How? Why is God love?"

Every child enters life with curiosity, seeking and

questioning. With great labor and financial cost, we educate children, only to eradicate this natural passion to question. Education is often that process of remembering and then regurgitating what has been memorized. Education is only one of the social means to smother the eternal child within the heart. Religion also shares in that repression when it makes the question or doubt a sin.

To propose the question mark as the new holy symbol for spiritual people will present some problems, since we have been educated to think of religion as having the answers instead of the questions. A truly great religion does not give answers so much as it raises great questions that challenge the believer to search inwardly for the answers. What is the meaning of life? Where am I going? Why do I suffer, and what is the meaning of the pain in my life? Are there "pat" answers, easily memorized, to such questions, or must each of us struggle within our hearts to live out the answers? A friend recently sent me a letter that had written across the top of the page a sentence that sounds very Zen. It read, "I owe everything to my teacher, he taught me nothing." Could we, in this period of renewed interest in religious education, offer a new catechism? It would be a handbook of religion filled with questions, but this new version would not have answers included! Such a teaching tool might once again awaken the natural childlike curiosity within each of us.

Naturally, to question the creeds we have been taught will be a difficult task because of our childhood religious formation. We have been taught that to question is to doubt and to doubt (to even have feelings of doubt) is sinful. Indeed, doubt is part of the mystery of searching, seeking—even seeking the Kingdom. As they say in the Orient—doubt leads to questioning, questioning leads to truth and truth leads to enlightenment. That is holiness. To ask questions is part of the
116

prayerful spirituality of any true seeker.

What effect would there be in our lives if our prayers contained more questions? Perhaps we would begin our prayers with the sign of the question, "Lord, am I in communion with you, with all of you, as I begin this prayer?" We could also end our prayers with the sign of the question, "Well, Lord, now that I come to the end of this time of speaking to you, how will you now speak to me in my life?" We could even trace over ourselves the sign of the question instead of the cross when suffering and difficulties, as well as joy, enter our daily lives. Instead of slavish surrender to pain, we ask, "Why and how can I use this experience for glory and for good?" When gifted with joy and blessings, instead of a mechanical "Praise God!" I ask, "Why, Lord? Why me? How can I use your gifts with deep gratitude, and how can others share in my gifts?" To pray in the sign of the question is to open the gates of heaven because it is to pray as a child prays.

The question mark is not only the prayer tool of the saint and mystic but also the creative tool of the artist, the genius, the explorer – those persons with whom society has been unsuccessful in suppressing the child within. Picasso and Einstein share in common with Edison, Columbus and the great mystics, a certain playfulness by which they question, like a child, the assumptions of life. The key to creativity and to saintliness is in remaining open, searching the unknown without fixed assumptions as to what one will find. As Matthew Fox says, "We experience the God we believe in, but rather, we should believe in the God we experience." When we use a question mark as a probing tool to test our experiences of love, nature and friendship, we discover God.

The child within us awakens each time we question life in a creative manner (the question mark is not only the holy sign of the child but can also be the

117

poisonous sign of the cynic who, in viewing life, asks the questions, "Is life really worth it?" or "Can anything good come from Nazareth?"). Creative questions that come from a youthful heart explore the meaning of persons and experiences. Such a heart is curious about relating these questions to life and discovering something that the heart did not know about itself before. For the young child the question is fun. Children play with questions as they play with toys – for the fun of it! The spiritual use of the question as a search for holiness should not be devoid of that element of mirth and fun. The presence of mirth is one of the infallible signs of the presence of the Divine Mystery. The question, as a child's toy, is one toy we should possess all our lives because it is an age retardant! As an adult toy, we should carry it to our graves.

This spirit of open-mindedness that is united with a sense of mirth is the means of "dying young as late as possible." In fact the concept of spirit itself is that very childlike quality. To question ourselves, life and God is to be spiritually young, and to be spiritually young is to be a mystic. Each of us is called to mysticism, to the daily experience of the Divine Mystery. We will miss that basic human vocation if we are afraid to be curious. We shall also miss that wholeness for which we were designed, that healthy holiness of the children of a holy and healthy God. How many persons die early but have a long wake? Sometimes thirty or forty years pass, before they are actually buried, after they have forgotten the secrets of staying young. The secrets are to have someone to love, some work for our hands, something to look forward to and to remain through all of life as childlike explorers by being persons who think critically.

Not only must we continuously ask questions, but we should learn how to ask the right questions. The use of the question can be a search for an answer, or

it can be the search for the problem. If we seek a solution to the problem, we can easily remain trapped in those tested and tried answers that may be part of the reason why the problem is still around. Searching for the problem is the beginning of the excitement of fresh discoveries and new solutions. A child is usually more concerned with the problem than with finding an answer. We are creative persons when we ask childlike questions. Frequently Jesus seemed to question a problem instead of proposing, or even seeking, a solution. That would be natural since he came to announce a New Israel, not to echo the old. His would be a New Kingdom with a new attitude of heart and a new solution to aged questions. The Samaritan woman at the well asked him a question, "Our fathers worshiped on this mountain, but you say that at Jerusalem is the place where one ought to worship?" Jesus said to her, "Woman, believe me, the hour is coming when neither on this mountain nor in Jerusalem will you worship the Father" (John 4:20-21). He went on to say that God is a spirit, and the persons who wish to worship him must not seek out some building or sacred mountain but rather look within their hearts. They must make those hearts prayerful places of spirit and truth. The question is not, "Where is the true temple?" but rather, "What is the temple?" The problem is not the geographic place of worship but worship itself.

May our use of the question mark as a religious sign open us to a year-round celebration of being gifted. Gifts come not only on Christmas but daily as we are showered with beautifully wrapped gifts. Some of them are wrapped in sorrow, some in laughter, some in ecstatic joy, some in sweat and some in confusion. We open these gifts of life with our holy question mark. With it we unwrap some gifts that are very old and some that are very new.

As we began this reflection on the spirit of the child,

we said that the question, as a religious sign, could be more powerful than the sign of the cross. Some who read this may have been disturbed by that remark, but let them remember that the sign of the cross is the great cosmic question mark. Why? For what reason? Unless we have learned to live in the pattern of Jesus, who questioned his life, social customs, environment and religious beliefs, the cross will not ask the most dynamic question of all history. It will be simply a hollow decoration.

# The Mother of All Prayer: Gratitude

In ancient Japan it is said that after a night of making love, the man had to write a poem so that when his lover awakened she might find the poem next to her sleeping mat. This ancient Japanese custom was intended to link together sensuality and love. The poem and the consideration behind its creation was a reassurance that the sexual exchange was a fruit of love and not just a "taking." The poem did not have to be a Longfellow epic. It could be a short three-lined Haiku poem like this one by Basho:

As bell tones fade
Blossom scents take up the ringing:
Evening shade!

The thanksgiving gift of the poem was but one way to assure the woman that she was truly loved. Not only women, but men as well, need to be frequently reassured that they are loved. Expressions like that of the lover's poem, expressions that are both thanksgiving and affection, are essential to any human love affair. They are equally essential in our love affair with God.

The late Rabbi Heschel said that prayers of gratitude, blessing prayers, are the place where heaven and earth meet. A sort of nuptial union were these expressions that celebrated rainbows and God, new shoes and God, fresh bread and God, as well as the ten thousand other such "marriages" between heaven and earth. This sort of prayer-poem served the same purpose as the poem left by the Japanese lover. The benedictions

123

or short prayers of gratitude, as brief as a Haiku poem, are central to Jewish spirituality. If we, as followers of Jesus, seek to follow him, we would do well to explore this aspect of Jewish spirituality which he, in his lifetime, expressed so well. As Messianic Jews, persons with Judaic roots and traditions, but for whom the Messiah has come, we should seek the spirituality of Jesus instead of a spirituality about Jesus. A dynamic part of our tradition of prayer is the Berakhot prayers or, as they are called, the benedictions.

The benediction prayer form was an ancient Jewish prayer form that was used by our Lord in his daily life. It was an important part of every meal and the Passover Meal in particular. At the Last Supper, we know that "he took bread; saying the blessing, he broke it. . . ." The Berakhot prayers were the environmental prayers of Jesus, a spirituality that touched every aspect of his life. Scholars believe that these blessing prayers appeared about the fourth century B.C. and soon became an important part of the daily spirituality of the Jewish people. They are short prayers, no longer than a sentence or two. Their purpose is thanksgiving and an awareness of the Divine Mystery in the most common aspects of life. An example of the benediction prayer used even today by the devout before eating bread is: "Blessed are you, Lord our God, King of the Universe, who brings forth bread from the earth."

These prayers are not an act of blessing God, since only God can bless. They are expressions of proclaiming the holiness of God. Such prayers are acts of lifting up the spirit in gratitude for some particular gift. Berakhot prayers are so numerous that they touch each and every aspect of life. A brief review of them only reveals the poverty of our prayer-life today. For example, there are praise-thanksgiving prayers for each act of taste — special prayers for the taste of bread, wine, cakes, fruits, vegetables, ice cream, fish and meat. This
124

incarnational spirituality has prayers for the gift of smell, prayers for the special smell of the bark of trees, scented woods, perfume, incense and fresh fruits. "Blessed are you, Lord our God, King of the Universe, who gives a pleasant scent to apples." There are prayers for sounds such as thunder, for good news and for unpleasant or sorrowful news. There are prayers of gratitude upon seeing natural manifestations like rainbows, sunsets, lightning, stars, deserts, mountains and trees blooming in the spring, and prayers for seeing a king or a scholar or holy person. There are benedictions for touch, such as the brief prayer of gratitude for a new garment when it is first worn, and there are prayers for anything new – a house, a pair of shoes, a book. There is also a benediction for washing one's hands (a religious deed always done before eating bread), and prayers said upon rising in the morning. These sunrise prayers of benediction speak of wonder and gratitude for the gifts of sight, life, clothing to wear and the ability to use one's arms and legs. These sunrise prayers are a sort of Japanese-Jewish love poem meant to reaffirm one's love affair with God. These are all expressions of the joyous thanksgiving for being alive. This has been a brief and inadequate summary of a deeply religious custom, but enough of a review to reflect upon the presence or absence of gratitude and appreciation in our lives.

We live in a secular world, in the midst of a society that is non-spiritual, as well as one not given to leaving poems on pillows. When we see a rainbow, we do not say, "Berakhot...Blessed be God...." Instead we say, "Wow, look at the rainbow!" Exclamations and slang, like "Isn't that neat!" have replaced expressions of gratitude and praise. A few relics of a former age do remain. Often people say a blessing before they eat, and there is also the ritualistic toast with a glass of wine on a special occasion. Other than these occasions, we

find a desert of devotion when it comes to pausing for prayer before the enjoyment of some common thing like a new pair of shoes. Even disregarding the absence of a spirit of prayer and the inability to live in the midst of wonder, we have so dulled our modern life that we find little joy in "just being alive." Instead of being filled with wonder and joy, our lives become a series of personal problems.

An ancient saying among the rabbis was, "A person who enjoys the pleasures of this world without a blessing is called a thief because the blessing is what causes the continuation of the divine flow into the world." The Japanese of olden times would have said the same: "A person who enjoys the pleasures of a woman without a poem is called a thief. . .and a fool!" We are surrounded with love and wonder, encircled by marvel and beauty. To use these, to enjoy them without returning some expression of thanks, is to be a thief and a fool. It is to take something which is gift and treat it as non-gift. We rob ourselves, not God, by such arrogance because when we become unaware, the divine flow ceases. Gifts dry up like a Kansas creek in August. To live lives of gratitude by frequent actions of lifting up the human spirit to the Source of all gifts is to continue the divine flow of love into your world and *the* world.

When thanksgiving is absent from our lives, the flow of divine energy ceases and our lives, as a result, become filled with troubles, trials and stress. As a result, we begin to wonder about our love affair with God as does any person whose relationship with another is devoid of gratitude and poetic praise. We all need to be reassured and to be thanked. The classic Jewish Berakhot prayers are always in the present tense, and that is important. "Blessed are you...who creates, who brings forth, who gives...." To pronounce such a blessing is to be reminded that the person is in
126

Lift up your hearts.
We lift them up to the Lord.
Let us give thanks to the Lord our God.
is right to give him thanks and praise.

the middle of the divine flow; that creation did not happen long ago, but rather is happening in the here and now! We can understand better Rabbi Heschel's statement that these benediction prayers are the place where heaven and earth meet, where God and clean hands meet, where God and fresh pears meet.

There is a story about a famous rabbi named Ben Zakkai who once asked his disciples a question: "Which is the worst quality a person should shun?" A student, Rabbi Simeon, responded, "To borrow and not repay!" Blessing or benediction prayers are expressions of gratitude for the continuous flow of the gifts of smell, taste, sound, sight, touch, and a reminder that we are not the owners of earth, but only its guests. We are stewards that have been loaned a multitude of marvels. Life is loaned to us and we have been loaned to one another. Mindful of that non-permanency, how else can

127

we respond but with gratitude? This Jewish concept of being aware that we live in debt for what has been loaned to us is also beautifully expressed by an ancient Aztec Indian prayer. This prayer from ancient Mexico, which also speaks of God's activity in the present, is addressed to God, whose name translated from Aztec means, "He in whose juice all of us grow."

Oh, only for so short a time have you loaned us to each other. Because you take form in your act of drawing us, and we take life in your painting us, and we breathe in your singing us. But only for a short time have you loaned us to each other. Because even a drawing cut in crystalline obsidian fades. And even the green feathers, the crown feathers, of the Quetzal bird lose their color, and even the sounds of the waterfall die out in the dry season. So, we too, because only for a short while have you loaned us to each other.

Thanksgiving is not a once-a-year holiday. Rather, thanksgiving is a way of life. Gratitude is the atmosphere that surrounds a person in love and is the environment for "natural" prayer. In our day-by-day lives we have the opportunity for ten thousand prayers. We need to find some modern and natural way to express gratitude and wonder. It might be of assistance to phrase our gratitude in a ritual form such as the Berakhot prayers. One could simply say, "Blessed be God who gives a parking place in front of the store." If a consciousness of gratitude is alive in our heart, a simple "ahhh..." could be a high prayer. Among the Sufis, the Moslem mystics, the name for Allah is "Ahhhhhhh."

As we reflect upon this prayerful expression, we

128

should remember that the purpose of the blessing is not ceremony but gratitude. Ceremony is performed for others and is primarily external. These blessings are internal and are performed for the sake of God. The benediction prayers are the turning of our attention toward God and are not intended to draw attention to ourselves. They are personal prayers and not an occasion to preach to others. These expressions are as personal as the love poem left by the Japanese lover. As such, they should reflect that sort of intimate personal relationship and not become bumper stickers.

Such prayers remind us that there is a difference between saying "thank you" and feeling thanks or gratitude. Prayers of gratitude tend to be intellectual when they come at formal ritual times. Benediction prayers, since they occur at the very moment of the experience, are directed towards what we are feeling. They are incarnational prayers that spring from the heart and not the head. They are love poems that are gifts of the moment and not debts of obligation.

As we reflect upon the numerous ways to be mindful of the divine flow, to be conscious of what has been loaned to us and to awaken to the ten thousand gifts of today, we will find ourselves with more gifts than we can unwrap. Among the multitude of gifts is one that is highly prized in today's world. Rare among us is the person who is satisfied. We seem to be constantly in need of something new, something different. Modern media have punctuated every aspect of life with commercials and their power to heighten our desires for "new and better" things.

The by-product of the benediction prayers is the gift of appreciation of what we already have and who we are. That by-product also includes the benefit of the love poem left on the pillow by the Japanese lover. We know that God has made love with us and we with God.

# The Sacred Art
# of Letter Writing

In the midst of the dreary, gray days between Christmas and Easter comes the scarlet feast of Valentine's Day. This often unappreciated feast day, like the cockroach, has survived the ravages of time and is still alive and well today. Valentine's Day is a festival of romance and friendship. We send greetings to sweethearts, friends and lovers. And of all the various greetings written on cards and letters, from the tender and affectionate to the humorous, the one that is foremost is "Be My Valentine." Outside of this festival, such affectionate tenderness is rare. Valentine's Day is very much a children's festival because children are more open and free with expressions of love than adults.

The tradition of sending letters and cards to friends on this feast is one of its greatest values. Letter writing is a human activity that is in grave danger. Like the bald eagle, letter writing is an "endangered" species. To write a letter takes time, not to mention at least 20¢ for postage. As a result, we find it easier to pick up the telephone and "reach out and touch someone." But, do we really "touch" them? A telephone call makes present to us the voice of the person, but lacks the magic of a letter. Valentine's Day holds great promise as a means of protecting, even promoting, the ageless art of letter writing. We need a feast that can do that.

Valentine's Day, or more correctly *Saint* Valentine's Day, is a holiday that is the result of the cross fertilization of the pre-Christian Roman feast of Lupercalia and the celebration of the Christian feast honoring an ear-

131

ly saint by the name of Valentine, beheaded in 270 A.D. Legend says that Valentine was a letter writer who would send messages of love and hope to his friends from his prison cell. The remembrance day of this early Christian martyr was united with the festival of the Romans, which was a lover's holiday. On Lupercalia, a festival of Pan, young people chose partners for the coming year (which began on March 1st in those days) and exchanged gifts as signs of affection. The two feasts became a single holiday that has lasted all these years and has grown in popularity with each passing age.

For the poor and the middle class in 1840, the holiday took on new life when the British issued the first postage stamp. Prior to that, the English had already replaced the giving of gifts on February 14th with the sending of notes or cards with messages of love and affection. The mid-nineteenth century saw the great expansion of the postal system for the ordinary person, which made it much easier to exchange valentines. By the time of the American Civil War, the feast had become so popular that a writer in a magazine in 1863 wrote, "Indeed, with the exception of Christmas, there is no festival throughout the world which is invested with half the interest belonging to this cherished anniversary."

Today, while we have the advanced technology necessary to zip letters all around the world, while we all are able to read and write...we lack the time to correspond with friends and family. We also lack time for un-hurried affection and romance, not to mention friendship. Because of this social situation, Valentine's Day is a marvelous opportunity to look at these two "endangered" human activities — letter writing and friendship. Our hectic, overworked and under-playful society has a deep hunger for friendship, for deep interpersonal relationships. Surveys show that over seventy percent of Americans recognize that they have

many acquaintances but few friends. And they acknowledge that this lack is a serious void in their lives. Most of our relationships with persons we call "friends" are superficial and fleeting. It appears that almost three-fourths of us are unwilling to commit ourselves to lifelong and deep friendships because they cost too much!

Friendship requires not only commitment, but also communication. Friendship feeds on a re-affirmation of the delicate bonds that unite, on a continuous flow of news about what we are thinking, about changes in our values and feelings — in brief, what is happening to the "inner" us. Communication is essential in this age of continuously changing values if friends are not to drift apart. Indeed, the telephone is a marvelous invention for that communication, and because of it we do tend not to write to each other as often as those who lived in previous ages. But as Andy Rooney (of "60 Minutes" TV fame) said in an article:

> No matter what the telephone company says, a phone call disappears into the air as soon as the receiver is put back on the hook. A good letter can last a lifetime. Some of my most precious possessions are letters that have been written to me in the past. I don't have a single memorable phone call stored in a box in my attic.

I agree with Andy. Fourteen years ago when I was on a pilgrimage of prayer that took me to India and the East, I remember my great joy when I picked up the mail that was waiting for me in Israel. I had only been away three months from the States, but the intense pleasure of those letters is still vivid in my memory. I read and re-read them. I carried them with me in my backpack the rest of my journey, even though space

in it was precious and allowed only for essentials. I saw those letters as sacraments, holy things, paper tabernacles that contained the love of my friends. I still have those letters today. It was there in Israel that I first became aware of the magical power of letters...that they were mystical! They were prayers! Without hesitation I can say to you that to write or to receive and read a letter is a form of prayer.

Letters as sacraments should not surprise us. An essential part of Christian worship is the reading of letters – the epistles of Paul, Peter and others. The Second Testament contains twenty-one letters which were originally sent to the early Christian communities. Then they were passed around to other communities and finally gathered officially with the Gospels into a book – the New or Second Testament. In one of those letters, Saint Paul's scribe who took down the epistle for him wrote, "Clearly you are a letter of Christ which I have delivered, written not with ink but by the Spirit...not on stone but in the flesh of the heart" (2 Corinthians 3:3).

You and I are meant to be "letters" to the world. People who "read" us receive a message from the Divine Mystery. Now, *there's* a delightful vocation – to be a sort of "valentine" from God to a love-hungry world! But if we are to be living, divine letters, "words made flesh," we, of all people, should keep alive and treat with respect the beautiful custom of letter writing. As we take time to do this, let us remember that such activity is always prayer. Let us remember that it is also prayer to receive and read a letter. Perhaps we could pause at the conclusion of having penned a note to a friend and trace the sign of the cross upon the letter to remind ourselves of this fact. Or, we could breathe part of our spirit into the envelope. More than just a puff of breath, we could send along with our message a part of our soul. Since love is invisible, some ritual
134

Blessed Archie:
I just loved your letter. I was so glad to hear from you.
I was afraid you would have trouble with

or sign helps us to remember what it is we are really sending when we send a letter to someone we love.

But what makes the sending or receiving of a letter a prayer? One of the letters that is read to us at Christian worship is from Saint John, the beloved. In it he wrote, "God is love." To send greetings of love, affection and affirmation is to "send God" to one another! To receive love through the mail is to receive a beautiful form of holy communion, for it is to receive the Divine Lover. It is almost instinctive, then, that we save and treasure letters. Besides being a form of incarnational prayer, letter writing is also a form of "wild life preserve" where endangered species are protected from destruction. In this case, what is protected and preserved is the expression of affection. We dare to say to friends in a letter what we might find embarrassing to say in person.

Usually a letter begins with the salutation "Dear." And personal letters usually conclude with the wish of "love." These two little four-letter words are in danger of becoming extinct. As the technological age expands, it seems that affectionate terms used in our communication are disappearing. I became aware of this while reading some old letters written to my great-grandparents. The letters were stored in an old iron box under the staircase of the family farm home. Only recently were they discovered. A letter to my Irish great-grandfather from his cousin in Deargroin, Ireland, dated January 17, 1876, began like this:

My dearly beloved cousin Thomas,

With sincere affection I avail the most pleasing opportunity of writing to you, hoping in the Divine Redeemer to find you and wife and family, together with all my beloved cousins in your vicinity. . .in a good and cheerful state of health. . . .

People a hundred years ago, lacking all our modern, time-saving devices, had both the time and desire to be more affectionate. Perhaps by the time another hundred years has passed, in the year 2084, we will begin letters by simply saying, "Thomas." "Dearly beloved," or even "Dear," will have disappeared from common usage in our letter writing.

As each Valentine's Day comes to us, we can use it as an occasion to reflect about that seemingly "unholy" activity of letter writing. We can look upon those letters we owe others — letters that should be written — not as burdens or unpleasant obligations that prevent us from watching television, but as an activity that keeps us human and also holy. The letters we write to those who are sick or elderly are acts of prayerful compassion. Our "thank you" notes should be viewed as Eucharistic, as thanksgiving prayer. Such letters of gratitude and appreciation provide us with wonderful opportunities to express our hearts' sentiments to a parent, child, lover or friend, instead of saying it to their coffin. Parents can use opportunities such as a son or daughter turning twenty-one, being married or starting a new career, to give a gift of their love, expressed in written words. Such a letter will be a treasure that the child, now a young adult, will keep for life. And for each of us who have parents who are still living, Valentine's Day, or any such occasion, would be a beautiful opportunity to incarnate, make concrete, our gratitude, love and appreciation for all that our parents have given to us.

While I will not deny that letter writing is somewhat an art form, it is really only expressing on paper what we would like to say to another face to face. The more we share feelings instead of facts, the more human is the letter and the more we send a gift of self. We should take time to respond properly to a letter, even if the person must wait many months to receive

it. I remember reading once that when St. Francis Xavier left for Japan and the Far East, St. Ignatius promised to write to him. St. Francis Xavier looked each day for that letter from Ignatius, and it finally came—

three years later! Postal service is considerably faster today than in the sixteenth century. So rather than write in haste, let us prayerfully send our love by mail in due time.

138

The renewal of Valentine's Day as a mystical celebration honoring correspondence could also encourage us to take the time necessary to maintain, energize and enjoy our existing friendships. It could encourage us to take the time necessary to move our relationships beyond the superficial to the substantial, and onward to the sacred. This February holiday should also remind us that you and I are, as St. Paul said, "...a letter of Christ...." Through the expression in our daily lives of patience, compassion, understanding and forgiveness, the love of God becomes a living reality in our world. In America we have the slang expression, "Do you read me?" What do others read when they read us? Emily Dickinson once wrote:

> This is my letter to the World
> That never wrote to Me –
> The simple News that Nature told –
> With tender Majesty.

What simple news does Nature tell with tender majesty? That news is what my "living letter" to the world should be. For written with tenderness in every leaf and mountain is the simple and sacred news of its Creator-God: "I love you."

# The Necessity of Idleness

"Idleness is the devil's workshop" is an expression quoted with such reverence that most people believe that it can be found in the Bible. It cannot be found there! While not an inspired verse, we live its message as if it were. To it we could add the words of Reverend Isaac Watts, "For Satan finds some mischief still for idle hands to do," or the words of another seventeenth century clergyman, Robert Burton, "Be not solitary, be not idle." These expressions are part of the formation of our personal theologies about time spent in prayer, retreat and play. They are part of the theology of an industrialized people.

Stop and reflect. Isn't idleness a sin? When was the last time you sat on your front porch for hours doing nothing? When was the last time you spent an entire day doing nothing of value? Ah, yes, few Anglo-Saxons of this century have had the faintest idea of what the inside of the devil's workshop looks like. It should not be overlooked that in our society people are punished with idleness – with solitary confinement! Strange that in our money-conscious times we resist being idle, since it doesn't cost us a cent. But the real cost of being idle is guilt.

Why do we keep busy? Is it because we do not want to feel guilty for wasting time? Most of us are behind in our work as it is, and if we waste time we are only that much more behind. For most of us wasting time is a cardinal sin. Whenever we become victims of "imposed idleness," like those times when we are stopped

in a long line of cars waiting for a stalled freight train, are we not upset, anxious and even angry? Part of the reason why idleness creates guilt is found in the meaning of the word. Originally the word meant "worthless." Those of us who are forced into idleness by sickness, retirement, freight trains or power failures feel worthless.

In an industrial society, idle people are looked upon as lazy, as parasites or even as dangerous. Ben Franklin summed it up in these words, "When men are employed, they are best contented...but on idle days they are mutinous and quarrelsome." We believe that idle minds are breeding grounds for impure thoughts and mutiny. Perhaps this is one reason why religious communities of both men and women attempt to keep their members constantly busy, always "on duty." Saint Paul also had ideas on idleness. In a rather negative statement about young widows, he tells Timothy, "They learn to be idle, wandering about from house to house, and not only idle, but gossips also and busybodies" (1 Tim. 5:13).

Today, unfortunately, we have become "busybodies" because we have *not* learned to be idle. Busy-minds, busy-hearts and busy-bodies all lack time for the natural joys of life. "Busybodies" are also sick bodies. As the Tao Te Ching of China says, "Always be busy and life is beyond hope..." (Ch. 52). While alcohol addiction is a great disease that has been and is the cause of untold destruction of homes, marriages, careers and life, we have another disease of equal harm. Alcoholism and drug addiction are seen as serious problems. The Church, the State and the business world support countless programs that offer cures for the alcoholic. But what about the "workaholic"? Here we see a radical difference. The Church, the State and the industrial-business complex reward with promotion, gifts and gold medals those addicts who make their
142

work their total and full-time occupation. Why do we lack programs to cure us of our addiction to work? How many recovered workaholics do you know? Have you, even for a fleeting moment, wondered if you are a work-addict? If so, answer these questions.

A. Are you able to visit without having to talk about your work?

B. Are you able to spend an entire day without a little "shot" of work?

C. Are you a closet worker? Do you take your work home with you, to bed with you? Do you "sneak work" – making play, prayer and leisure laborious?

D. Do you, when forced by some circumstance to sit and do nothing, find that the palms of your hands sweat and little crawly creatures can be felt in your pants?

To lack meaningful work to perform in life is to be cursed, but to be unable to stop working is an even greater curse. Anyone who is seriously interested in becoming holy, interested in prayer or the spiritual journey, must learn on occasions to be idle without guilt. We should learn to recognize how deep is our social discrimination against wasting time. As hard-working, decent Christian or Jewish folk, we look down with disdain on those who are idlers.

While on vacation, a successful businessman visited an Indian village. As he walked along, he saw a man lying under a tree, doing nothing. The businessman stopped and said, "Hey, Chief, don't you think it's time to be up and about – doing something productive?" The man under the tree looked up and answered, "Why?" The businessman said, "Why? So you can get a job, earn some money and make something of yourself." The man under the tree smiled again and said, "Why?" Now an-

noyed, the businessman replied, "Why...don't be so dumb. So you can make money, start a savings account and then someday you can retire and enjoy life." The man under the tree answered, "I'm enjoying it right now!"

For us, that's impossible! To enjoy life now is also against the rules of the game of life. We are not supposed to enjoy life now. Today we are to work hard, and then sometime in the future we can enjoy being idle. Since childhood we have been taught to postpone enjoyment. And because we are a people of habit, postponement becomes a life pattern. If retirement ever comes to us, we usually feel worthless, because we are non-productive. We have also forgotten how to enjoy the present moment through a lifetime of postponement. Those of you who agree with the truth of these statements will also agree that it's time for new slogans. So haul down the sign that reads, "Idleness is the devil's workshop," and replace it with, "Idleness is God's playroom."

Students in an adult kindergarten – in God's playroom – are those who can, on occasion, be idle. Kindergarten is a marvelous model for all learning, since it is a combination of play and study. In being able to spend time doing nothing, being idle, we learn a valuable lesson. What we learn is that we are grown-up children, persons who are valuable not for what we do, but for whom we are. Dorothy Parker once said, "Four be the things I am wiser to know: idleness, sorrow, a friend and a foe." The ability to be idle teaches us that personal value is not found in the industrial sense of profit, but in simply being who we are: unique, creative, original works of divine art. A Picasso painting doesn't have to do anything; its great value is found in its "is-ness."

Being students in the playground-school of idleness teaches us the most perfect prayer of gratitude, the en-

144

joyment of the gift. When we can sit and stop working, we find that the wine tastes better, the sun is brighter and the song of birds is clearer. Because of idleness, we are more aware of all of life, and it takes on a greater charm. A mystic is one who experiences the Divine Mystery. Being idle allows us to taste, see, feel and hear the Divine Presence. Whenever you "play around" with a guitar, a softball bat or with writing an original poem, you enter the realm of the mystical. Whenever you are able to reject feelings of guilt and can enter fully into such "irresponsible" activities as puttering around, tinkering or even poking along, you are in God's playroom... and your prayer-room. It is good to be lazy on certain days, to be idle at certain times in each day. Without space or time to waste, how can creativity, dreams or prayers ever be possible?

In the play *Romeo and Juliet* Mercutio says to Romeo, "True, I talk of dreams which are the children of an idle brain." Prayers are also the children of an idle brain. Idleness is not only God's playroom, it is also the Holy of Holies, the residence of the Mystery. The great and beautiful temple of Yahweh in Jerusalem was the center of all worship. And, at its very center was the Holy of Holies, the dwelling place of God. So sacred was this tabernacle of the temple that only the high priest was allowed to enter it – and then only once a year, on the Day of Atonement. Behind the heavy veil that covered its entrance was a room that measured 30-by-30 feet. And, what was in the Holy of Holies? Nothing – it was entirely empty!

God dwells in a mystical manner, in empty, silent spaces. Should it surprise us hard-working "busybodies" of a technological world that we find God absent from our busy, crowded, never-empty lives? Today, we insist that our new churches be multipurpose. We hate empty, unused space, even if it is God's space. Our worship, as well, is constantly busy with words, song and
146

action. We are uncomfortable with idle worship, with silent inactivity. The prayer of the heart, meditation, is difficult because it is time spent in an empty, idle, non-productive manner. Other forms of prayer allow for addition: fourteen psalms recited, three pages of scripture read, five decades of the rosary prayed. But silence, how do you total up silence? Each time we still ourselves and do nothing, each time we pray idle prayer, we move closer to the Divine Mystery that dwells within our personal Holy of Holies. Unless we can learn to waste time, we will never be happy or holy people.

Is this call to be idle, to "waste" time, in our busy contemporary life, unrealistic? In a world where usually both husband and wife must work outside the home, where the demands of family, church, community and neighbors are constantly at our door, we must wisely budget our time or we will pay the cost. The Sabbath, the day of rest (idleness), must be used to do the laundry, clean the house, mow the lawn, wax the car, visit our parents, do our shopping...and the list goes on. Where is the time we are supposed to waste? Who among us can run away from our responsibilities and become slow-moving hill-Billies or hill-Betsys? Well, we know that we can do several things with time — we can "kill" it, "waste" it, "spend" it and we can "enjoy" it. Part of our anxiety about wasting time is well-founded. What if time is but a code-word for life? Who wants to waste life? If time is life, then we might examine our activities to see if any of them are forms of being idle.

For example, is watching television, that great pastime which amounts to about thirty-five hours a week for the average American, idleness? Watching television, that marvelous gift of this century, can be many things. If we watch one program after another instead of choosing a "special" program, it can be a

means to simply "spend" time, an avoidance of being creatively idle. Watching a "soap" or an afternoon of sports, while being enjoyable, is not often idle time. Idle time is re-creative; it is the enjoying of time, ourselves and all we include in the magic word, "Life." The inner person is renewed by contact with the unproductive, empty time where God dwells.

To engage in that "old-fashioned" activity of going for a drive can be a taste of idleness. "Going for a drive" is not going anyplace, since we lack a destination. The car ride is a form of idleness in motion that is much akin to the great American invention, the rocking chair − which allows one to be idle, yet on the move! Going for a ride or for a walk allows for the casual conversation, the wasted talk, that is so essential for love. Fishing is another form of idleness − that is, if it really doesn't make any difference whether you catch anything or not. Dancing might also be classified as "idle movement" since you are not going anywhere productive. Whenever we play sports − not to win, but just to play − we are in a form of idleness. And, of course, another idle sport is soaking in a hot bathtub. These are but a few of the ways to be idle that are a part of the human enjoyment of life − an enjoyment that is to be tasted now, tonight or today. The test of "idle" time is, "Am I more alive, more alert, more relaxed, more holy (even if I don't realize it at the time), as a result of doing nothing?"

If we are to be idlers instead of "busybodies," we will have to use discipline to create spaces and times for the doing of nothing. We will have to adjust our schedules. On a day off, when you have drawn up a list of "musties" (those things that *must* be done), sit down and cut it in half! Then, whatever you are doing, whether the laundry or weeding the garden, try to do it in a lazy, idle way. Take your time, refuse to set a deadline and then taste fully whatever it is that

148

you are doing. Slowly we can un-educate ourselves about idle time and begin to enjoy it more and more. Just sitting and visiting opens doors and windows that reveal our feelings, doubts and dreams. Such insights into one another cannot be programmed into the famous, "I-think-we-ought-to-have-a-talk" sort of thing.

If we wish to be idlers, we will have to turn off the inner critic and leave the unwashed dishes in the sink, the lawn unmowed and last week's dust on the picture frames if we are to have any time for doing nothing.

Don't let the "musties" run your life. Learn to govern yourself (simply another way of saying "be disciplined"). Self-government or discipline will be necessary if you are to set aside time each day for prayer, especially silent prayer. And the more you can create an environment in your home that encourages the pleasures of idleness, the easier it will be. How blessed is the person who has a life companion, friend or lover who is an idler. While talking about being blessed, it could be proposed that an addition be made to the list of the nine beatitudes that Jesus gave to us in his famous Sermon on the Mount. The tenth beatitude would be, "Blessed are the idlers for they shall enjoy God...and life."

# Music: Gift from the Gods

Can you imagine what the Christmas Season would be like without music? If *White Christmas* or *Silent Night* and the other traditional songs were removed from the holiday season, it would be a very hollow holiday. Part of the original Christmas celebration was the music of the angels over the shepherded hills of Bethlehem. *Glory to God in the Highest* was played and sung by the Cosmic Archangel String Band and Flying Glee Club. This was only right and in keeping with tradition. Among the traditions of the villages of ancient Palestine was that of music surrounding the birth of a child. As the time of the birth drew near, the village notables and the town musicians would gather outside the home to await the great event.

The birth of the infant Jesus to Joseph and Mary happened while they were far away from their village, but the tradition was continued as a Cosmic Angelic Band performed. With real stars as performers, they filled the stillness of the night with joyous music. Without any doubt, at the birth of *every* child, the heavens open up and the earth is flooded with divine music. Let those who have ears listen!

But music is not restricted only to times of birth. Music is an essential part of life itself and forms an important aspect of all celebrations. At the truly human times, and therefore the sacred times, we celebrate by song and music. Music and religion have been companions since the most ancient days, perhaps since the beginning of time. We know that the people whose lives

form the web of all the Scriptures had music as an important part of their lives. We possess the words to their songs even if we do not know the melodies, as in the psalms. They made music at weddings, funerals, births and holy days, while they worked and when they went to battle. King Saul was relieved and quieted from his mad rages by the beautiful music of David's harp. The Prophet Elisha, when he needed to know the will of God, called for a musician to assist him in bringing forth a prophetic inspiration.

Previous to our modern age, only the very rich or royal people, such as King Saul, had musicians at their constant beck and call. Today, we are surrounded by a wide variety of musicians through radio, television and recordings. When we are in need of music all we have to do is flick a switch, and we are royally entertained. Since the presence of music is so common in our day, we can easily forget that it is a sacred manifestation, and that music can be prayer and worship. We recall that Saint Augustine once said, "He who sings, prays twice." We can also add to that observation, "He or she who listens to music, prays twice!"

Music is the sound of heaven, and that is why it is a double-prayer. Music is the harmony of chords that easily could be perpetual discord. The laws that govern the composition and playing of music are the same as those that govern the universe — harmony! In all the ancient traditions it was the gods that brought music and musical instruments to the earth from heaven. Music was a companion to the Holy Ones — Krishna with his enchanted flute, the god Pan with his pipes and Apollo with his harp — because music proclaims the mystery of the divine. Whenever you play it or are involved in it, even by listening, you are caught up in primal prayer. Jeremiah, Buddha and Hosea are called Prophets of the Most High, but so are Cole Porter, Stravinsky, Mozart and Willie Nelson! All music can
152

be sacred — rock-and-roll, classical, jazz, country western and ragtime — not simply "churchy" music. Music is not the handmaiden of religion — music is religion!

As people of an electronic entertainment age we, unfortunately, tend to be listeners more often than per-

formers of music. Listening to music is prayer, but to make music is a deeper mystical communion. As often as it is possible, we should "make music" as we "make love" — as integral parts of being human and therefore holy people. It takes courage and discipline to make music — to sing or play an instrument. Few of us are

skilled musicians, but we are all musicians to some degree. If we could begin to sing to ourselves in private, and to sing with others in communal settings, we might find it easier than we thought. By singing we can express our deepest feelings of joy or sorrow. We don't need to memorize other people's songs; we can make up our own! We did it as children, playfully singing our own original songs to ourselves. The talent is still there, even if it is buried beneath layers of sophistication. One way we can make music is by allowing ourselves to be in harmony with the experiences of life around us. Whenever we are in communion with creation, we are in the midst of a living song – the creaking of the limbs of trees or the humming of the wind in telephone wires, the songs of birds or the chanting of insects on a summer evening, the melody of rain on the roof – all creation is music. Besides these sorts of sounds and melodies there are also the sounds of the tea kettle on the stove, the hot hiss of grease or the swish of the broom, all forming the music of life.

But if we are to hear these sounds of life-music and enter into them, we will need to learn the art of "silent music." Silence is also a form of music. When we are able to create islands of quiet and solitude in the midst of our busy-busy lives, we are gifted by the awareness of life-music. We discover to our surprise that our bodies themselves are musical. They are rhythmic systems of pulses, beats and cadences all in harmony with an unheard mystical melody. Silent music gives us time to be in tune with that inner melody which resonates with the cosmic melody. As Kabir, the Moslem mystic from India, said, "Listen, friend, this body is His dulcimer. He draws the strings tight, and out of it comes the music of the inner universe...The Holy One is the only One who can draw music from it." When we allow our bodies to become instruments by taking time to hear silent music, we will experience

harmony all around us. Being part of the continuous concert of creation, we will discover that we are growing in health and holiness.

In the ancient days, medicine and music were co-workers. Since the arrival of modern science we have discarded music as a medicine. Today we would be shocked if the doctor came to see us and, sitting on the side of the bed, began to make music as a way to heal us. The philosopher, Pythagoras, used to prescribe a daily diet of music for the health of his followers. Until the nineteenth century, music was routinely used to treat mental depression. But this was "live" music, which has magical powers not found in recorded music. Though we may lack a live musician in our homes, let us not hesitate to listen to recorded music, and allow it to put us in harmony after the discords of daily life have caused a loss of inner balance.

Though we are surrounded by radios and record players, we should still make music ourselves. Music is an important part of public worship. We have all been encouraged to sing, the old and the young, and not to allow a professional choir to overshadow this natural human ability. But after years of practice we still find it difficult. Perhaps one reason is that singing is not an integral part of our daily lives. We are not a people who sing very often. A few echoes of former times are heard when *Happy Birthday* or our *National Anthem* are sung, but these are only remnants of a quaint and delightful custom. If singing in church is to be natural and full-hearted, we need to sing at other times – at the family table, in bars and whenever we gather to celebrate the special events of our lives. If this is to happen, we will have to learn how to be unconscious of self, which happens to be one of the primary lessons of any good spirituality. Those who sing from their hearts instead of their vocal cords are as free as children again. Musicians play instruments as children play – forgetting the

155

self.

Holy people, fools and children sing to themselves in the midst of daily activities. We need to sing as freely as St. Francis of Assisi. He called himself the Troubadour of God and loved to sing along with the birds or with Brother Wolf, unconcerned about the sound of his voice. You might say, "Wolves don't sing." But Michael Fox in his book *The Soul of the Wolf* says that when wolves howl it is often to express their unity and kinship through song! God gave distinctive voices to the wolf, the crow and other creatures, but that doesn't prevent them from using that voice in song. Take courage, and begin to sing. Forget what may have been said to you when you were in grade school: "Whisper the words and smile a lot." Regardless of what the local or family critics have said about your voice, it is the one that God gave you, and the one that God wishes to hear.

From ancient Russia comes a story about a monastery renowned for its marvelous music and chanting. One day, the monks learned that the Czar of all Russia was coming to pay a visit. With long hours of practice they prepared the music for the Sacred Liturgy, wanting it to be perfect for the Czar. In that monastery was one brother who had the worst voice in all of holy Russia. The abbot ordered the brother, under the vow of obedience, not to sing, lest his voice ruin the music. The day of the Czar's visit arrived, and the Sacred Liturgy was overwhelmingly beautiful. The poor brother was swept away by the enchanting music, the flickering candles, the golden vestments and the clouds of incense, and he began to sing. His voice rose above the choir, and it was terrible! After the Czar had departed, the abbot, in a rage, ordered the brother to keep a fast of bread and water and to sleep on the floor of his cell for thirty days. That night, Christ came in a vision to the abbot. He told the abbot, "Today, in

heaven, as we listened to the usual sounds that rise up from earth, we heard among them one voice filled with love and great devotion. All of heaven stopped to listen to such a magnificent voice. Then, to our surprise, we saw how you punished that brother who sang with such a full heart. Father Abbot, it is our wish that *you* keep the fast and sleep on the floor." The story ends when the abbot gave the brother his own bed, and never again did he forbid anyone to sing.

As the Russian story shows so well, the privilege of singing is not confined to those with melodic voices. It is part of our holy inheritance to lose ourselves in the joy of making music, "playing" instruments and "playfully" singing, and in that lively act to make God present in our lives. Emmanuel is another name for music; Emmanuel, God-among-us, is what happens whenever we listen to or make music.

Let us create a melody to decorate our homes in festive seasons and celebrations. May it surround our tables at our feasting. May it comfort us in sadness and calm our troubled hearts in times of confusion. Let music be with us in all seasons. May it awaken spring and season the seeds we plant in our gardens. May music be shade in the heat of summer and a tonic at picnics. May it be an added color to autumn and warmth to winter. As we make it our constant companion, we will find ourselves becoming a part of the harmony it brings, until we are enveloped in the Cosmic Song.

# The Love of Death and Life

"The man who loves his life loses it," said Jesus. And we can rephrase the continuation of that saying, "...while the man who hates his life..." to read "...while the man who loves death...will preserve his life!" But to love death sounds devilish because we have been trained from early childhood to love life and protect it. The paradox is, nevertheless, that unless we can have a love for death, we shall be unable to truly love life.

When we listen to the words of Christ, we find that death and dying are interlaced continuously with his philosophy of life. In his invitation to follow him, he sums up this theme when he says, "If anyone wishes to come after me, let him deny himself...for he who would save his life will lose it, but he who loses his life for my sake will find it" (Matt. 16:24-26). Our modern religious motivation is centered in the celebration of life and abounds in themes like resurrection, joy, new life and being born again. We seldom hear about death and its necessity (its essential necessity) for resurrection! The subject of death, like its twin, discipline, is untouchable in our society. This is not a new manifestation; it has been around for a long time. In fact, the Irish have an old expression about themselves that goes, "The Irish would rather die than talk about death." What is new, however, is our manner of dealing with the fear of death. Instead of taboos, superstitions and the rituals dealing with the dead, we who live today handle our fears by silence and denial. Rollo May has said that for us death is pornography;

159

it is the unmentionable dirty word!

Strangers in our midst, then, are the disciples of life, for to be a disciple of him who called himself Life is to keep the thought of death before our minds day and night. If we keep the reality of death before our eyes daily, we will be able to discharge our duties in a faithful manner. It will also make us alert spiritually, and so able to avoid a multitude of disasters in our lives. None of us should take today for granted! Each day must be lived as if it were the last day, and so it will be lived with respect and with great enjoyment. Beware of the thought, "I will live a long life." Such thinking is indeed dangerous since it breeds indulgence and gives an excuse to dissipate our energy. Such thinking allows the postponing of holiness and growth until tomorrow: "Be constantly on the watch! Stay awake! You do not know when the appointed time will come!" (Mk. 13:33-37). Are these words of a Western gunslinger or a samurai warrior? They sound like it, don't they? We know whose words they really are, and we can consider the reality of how such words are lived out each time we see a crucifix.

So, we are invited to a love affair with death. We await the "appointed time" as we await the arrival of a special letter from a good friend—with expectation! Such watchfulness has the power to activate talents and skills that would normally require long training to bring into perfection. A Zen story speaks about this mystery.

Once a long time ago in Japan, there was a great swordsman who finally became a teacher in the art of swordsmanship. His name was Ta'ji'ma-nokami. One day there came to him a young man who was a guard at the palace of the shogun, the military governor. The man wished to become a student under the Zen master and to learn the art of swordsmanship. But the old master said to him, "As I observe, you seem to be a master of the art yourself; pray tell me, before we enter

160

into the relationship of teacher and pupil, to what school do you belong?" But the man replied, "I am ashamed to confess that I have never learned the art." At this the Zen master became very disturbed, thinking that the man was attempting to fool him. It was apparent to his skilled eye that this young man who stood before him requesting training was already a master. But the man only denied again that he had ever studied the art of swordsmanship and said that he had no intention of making a fool of the teacher. To this, the sword master replied, "If you say so, then it must be true; but still I am sure that you are master of something, although I do not know what it is." The young man answered by saying, "Yes, if you insist, I will tell you. When I was a boy, I dreamed of becoming a samurai, a great warrior, and I realized that if this was my dream then I must never have any fear of death. Since those first days, I have grappled with death until it is no longer an issue. Death ceases to worry me. May this be what you are referring to?" And Ta'ji'ma' jumped up and exclaimed, "Exactly, that is what I mean. I am glad that I made no mistake in my judgment. For the ultimate secrets of swordsmanship also lie in being released from the thought of death. I have trained hundreds of my pupils along this line, but so far none of them really deserve the final certificate for swordsmanship. You are in need of no technical training, young man, you are already a master!"

The young man was a master because he had been freed from the thought of death (meaning the fearful thought) as he himself said, "Death ceases to worry me!" Like the man in the story, you will become a master of life when you have been liberated from the fear of death. Then your spiritual powers will bloom into fullness as you walk in the footsteps of the Lord of Life who himself balanced life and death with a holy indifference. "Do not be afraid of those who kill the body

161

but cannot kill the soul" (Matthew 10:23). This indifference to death is but another form of the skill and art of poverty, of detachment. Fear of death is a thought, an attitude of the mind, and as such it is a possession that can be given away. Like other possessions that limit life, when this fear is given away, you are free to perform wonderful deeds! You will consider every day of your life precious, and this being so, you will extend yourself beyond your own limitations. At the same time, tremendous energy will rush into your daily life, allowing you to take it seriously. The result is the ability to separate the essentials of life from the non-essentials, and that is the heart of poverty and simplicity. For as Jesus said, "Life is a greater thing than food and the body more than clothing" (Lk. 12:23).

A love of death and a love of simplicity are in reality the same love. When we stop clinging to persons or possessions, we are experiencing an act of dying. Such letting go of attachments is not a penance but a liberation. If we know what is essential in life, the process is not that difficult. There is a story about a very holy rabbi that may clarify this point.

Some people from the United States were traveling in Poland. As they passed through a certain village they were told that in it there lived a very holy rabbi who had made the village his home for most of his life. So the people came to see the holy man, and upon entering his home they were struck by the starkness of the dwelling. A simple sleeping mat, a table and a bench at which the rabbi sat studying the Scriptures were the only furnishings that could be seen. The visitors asked, "Rabbi, where is your furniture?" And, looking up from his reading, he said, "Where is *your* furniture?" And they answered, "Our furniture? Why should we have any furniture with us? We are only passing through here!" And the rabbi replied, "Well, so am I!"

When we are able to die to possessions, to be freed

from our attachments, we will know how much "furniture" to carry with us as we are passing through life. We will not make the mistake of burdening ourselves with anything that is unnecessary. Together with a certain freedom we will also find that our enjoyment of life will have greatly increased. We will be able to take delight in simple things — a shared cup of tea, a fresh morning sunrise, the first signs of spring or a conversation with a friend. All these and many other delights will suddenly be illuminated with splendor from within once they are labeled, "for today only!" Freedom and splendor from within will be joined by appreciation and gratitude, making all of life a joyful experience. But without a mindfulness of death, these essential qualities will be absent. Death and its companions — separation, loss, retirement, old age, the appearance of gray hairs and wrinkles in our skin — are a holy mystery. Death and old age are not problems to be solved; they are mysteries akin to the Divine Mystery, and as such they require not a solution but rather a life response.

If we desire to make a wholehearted response to death and to life, we shall, like the man who dreamed of being a samurai warrior, have to learn how to grapple hand-to-hand with the mystery of death (while being cautious so as not to become insensitive by overexposure to death in the media — the nightly viewing of death in national and international disasters). And, with courage, we shall wrestle with death as it enters our personal lives in the death of friends and members of our families. With sensitivity and courage, we will also learn to reverence death as we encounter it in nature — in the plants that die and in the experiencing of the cycles of winter and spring. The news of death should call forth a response of reverence, if not awe and wonderment. For if we meet the holy mystery of death in these ways, we need not fear that we shall become co-conspirators in the crime of the denial of death.

164

Life and death, like opposing powers, pull separately at each of our arms. We are pulled apart by the tension of these two mighty mysteries. We become like the strings of a musical instrument which, when the tension is correct, begin to vibrate with a divine music. But if we deny death and fearfully shut it out of our lives, the polarity is lost, and there is no creative tension. Without tension there is no music, and where there is no music, there is boredom. Being bored with life is an increasingly prevalent sickness. Bored people, who are also boring people, seek more and more stimulants to cure their sickness. And so, our lives sicken when we have refused to have a love affair with death. For people who cannot love death, tragically and ironically, cannot love life either.

# Conclusion:
# The Best-Kept Secret


In the beginning, when all was empty and void,
God's Spirit-Wind, restless and playful,
swept over the Sea and was captivated by her beauty;
she quivered and awakened at his touch.
Barely breathing, the Spirit
whispered gently as a breeze;
but the Sea did not answer, for she knew no words.
So the Spirit taught her the speech of Heaven,
and she was moved to her very depths with love
and sang to him in the language he had taught her
as he murmured to her of his love.
Gently they merged, and from that union
came a beautiful daughter whom they called Earth.
The Sea taught her daughter the language of Heaven,
and the Spirit, the Sea and Earth were one.

Eons of full moons rose and set,
until one day Earth gave birth to twins,
and she called them Adam and Eve.
The children played in the lap of their mother the Earth
on the sands where their grandmother Sea
embraced her daughter.
And they listened to their grandmother as she spoke,
"Swish-swash, swish-swash, swish-swash,"
and they were filled with peace.

Full moons by the millions rose and set,
and the children of Adam and Eve
began to move from the Sea.
166

Deep in the jungles they went,
and over the mountains and into the plains,
until they were so far away
that their grandmother's voice was gone.
No longer could they hear her ageless song —
the ceaseless harmony, the throbbing beat —
"Swish-swash, swish-swash,"
and they became greatly fearful and ill of heart.

As they huddled in fear, they cried with a single voice,
"Let us go back to our grandmother Sea
and our hearts will heal." But one spoke
whose name is lost in history.
"No, we must stay," he said. "Last night in a dream
I was shown a round box that held
the voice of the Sea. It was sacred,
a house designed by the Spirit.
'Build me this tabernacle,' He said."
And the children did as they were told —
and that is how the Drum came to be.

What joy they felt as the pounding of the surf
and the throb of the waters
and the voice of the grandmother
spoke to them through the Spirit-Drum,
"Swish-boom, swish-boom, swish-boom."
Far inland from the Sea they heard again
the heart-throb of creation; as they circled
the tabernacle of the Spirit, a single heartbeat
echoed in their breasts.

And the Drum became the first gift of the Spirit
when he came to his children, not as fire or wind,
but as rhythm, the pulse of their lives.
This was the primal liturgy,
the song of the Sea and the Spirit,
sung before the Earth came into being.

And the first priests were those who played
the Spirit-Drum and called up the voice
of the Spirit, the Sea and the Earth —
the Timeless Trinity.

Thousands of full moons rose and set,
and War came to live among the children of Earth.
War saw the magic of the Spirit-Drum,
saw its holy power to make many into one —
and War coveted the Drum.
So War told the children he was holy,
and they said, "Yes, you too may use the Drum."

Once-fearful folk, afraid to die,
heard "Holy War's" rhythm of hate, and joined
in a single body as they marched to battle
with the throbbing of the Drum,
"Courage-courage-courage; courage-courage-courage."
And the warriors were filled
with the power of the Drum,
its message now misused by the violence of War.

Earth-children sometimes grew weary of War
and banished him for various lengths of time,
but they missed the thrill of danger
and the drunken joy
when War marched home victorious
with prisoners locked in chains, so comical to see,
with wild animals captured in far-off lands
and the Drum singing,
"We won, we won, we won!"
So to fill the void when War was away
they invented the Circus.

With clowns to laugh at and wild beasts to astound
and high-wire acrobats with the courage of heroes,
the Circus delighted the hearts of the children.

169

And Circus said, "Please give me the Drum to play!"
And the drummers ordained the Circus,
and it became holy, too.

Then hundreds upon hundreds of full moons later,
solemn symphony orchestras
and jazz bands and rock groups came, hats in hand,
begging for the Drum.
So it came to pass that the most ancient and
sacred instrument, the mother of music,
was excommunicated from the Church!
The Drum was banished from worship — "Unworthy,
unfit, too sensual, too secular," they said.

Here ends this Genesis Tale — but within it is hidden the best-kept secret of Heaven, the divine comedy that plays itself out with silent laughter every day. The Ten Thousand Things, like the Drum, which once were most sacred, have now become most secular! This is how God dwells among us without causing fright: by becoming so un-Godlike that we forget. We find our lives enriched, but do not recognize our Benefactor!

The challenge of the saints of the twenty-first century is to begin again to comprehend the sacred in the Ten Thousand Things of our world; to reverence what we have come to view as ordinary and devoid of the Spirit. There is not a single vocation among us which was not once a priestly one — father, mother, soldier, doctor, teacher, nurse, artist, builder of houses and planter of seeds — all of them were ordained by God. And the daily actions of our lives — from making dinner to making love — are as sacred, as holy as the Drum. And music — ah, music...whatever its style or form — isn't it the Primal Pentecost? Every song of life is an Emmaus; when tone and tempo are one in harmony, we hear the Spirit.

# Other Books by the Author

## Prayers for the Domestic Church

This re-edited edition of a popular collection of 120 blessing and ritual prayers and 12 essays brings into focus the sacredness of such varied areas of life as sickness and death, holy days and holidays, daily personal prayer and a whole spectrum of everyday experiences.

## Twelve and One-Half Keys

Spun with a thread of magic, these 12½ delightful tales touch chords within that unlock doors of perception, bringing healing and opening the gates of paradise.

## The Ethiopian Tattoo Shop

A collection of 22 challenging, often humorous, always intriguing parable-stories for the searching heart.

## Pray All Ways

This collection of reflections on a modern mysticism suggests how we can pray with our whole person – with eyes, nose, feet. . .and at times we might not think were prayerful.

## Sundancer

An original fable which deals with life's most ancient riddle, touching at the heart of all the great religious traditions as it speaks of life, death and freedom.

## Prayers for the Servants of God

A collection of original prayers and essays for presiders, deacons, lectors, eucharistic ministers, religious educators and many others who serve God's people; prayers for private use, before and after ministering, meeting and various rehearsals and practices.

For further information
contact your local bookstore
or write directly to:
Forest of Peace Books, Inc.
Easton, KS 66020
913-773-8255

As Confucius
might say,
"Here's
1,000 words
about the
author."

Thank you
for your
company as
together we
have shared
the ideas
and visual
parables
of this
book.

peace+

**RECEPTIONIST**—mechanical Contractor located in Executive Park, has an immediatel opening for an experienced receptionist. Send resume to FOLEY CO. 7501 Front St. KCMO 64120

**RECEPTIONIST-MONDAY** thru FRIDAY 9 to 5:30, 913-262-5050

**RECEPTIONIST**—Must be able to type minimum of 60 wpm, answering phones, greeting clients, excellent company benefits. Call for appt, 525-0611-ask for Carol

### Receptionist/Gen. Office
Immediate opening for receptionist with:
- Accurate typing 55 wpm
- Good figure aptitude
- Professional front desk appearance
- Mature attitude
- Ability to handle variety
- Organized & follow through

816-421-1380

### RECRUITER
For Private Liberal Arts College. Starting immediately, service to KC area. experience preferred. Salary negotiable, call 816-736-5741 or write Director of Admission Tarkio College, Tarkio, Missouri 64491

### RENTAL AGENT
Office orientated, person who likes to meet the public, excellent salary & benefits, must be willing to work Sats. & 1/2 days Suns. President Garden Apt Complex, 8229 Troost, 444-5552

**REPORTER-PHOTOGRAPHER** for Platte County area. Beats include county court & schools. Lay-out experience helpful. For appointment call 781-1044.

Research

See our ad under Litigation Research in today's classified section.

### CONTROL DATA TEMPS

**RESTAURANT** ANNIE'S SANTA FE now hiring cocktail waiters/waitresses. Apply 2-4 pm M-F, 11855 W. 95th, OPK

**RESTAURANT** Assistant Manager with some waiter & fine dining room experience. Jasper's Restaurant, 405 West 75th Street

**RESTAURANT** Bennigans is looking for energetic people to hire as waiters/waitresses, hosts/ hostess, service assistant & cooks. Apply 2-4pm 5540 E. Bannister Rd. KCMO 966-8549   EOE

**RESTAURANT**—Cooks-experienced breakfast and dinner, bus persons, cashier/hostess/host. Apply in person, 7 Arches Restaurant, Best Western Stadium Inn, 7901 E. 40 Hwy.

**RESTAURANT-HARDEE'S** is now accepting applications for part time & full time positions for days & evenings. Please inquire at 79th & Quivira, Lenexa, Ks

**RESTAURANT HELP** Brown's Chicken now accepting applications for


**RESTAURANT-Fanny's** is now accepting applications for Assistant Captains. Apply in person 11-4 pm. M-F. 3954 Central. KC Mo

**RESTAURANT—THE COPPER OVEN RESTAURANT** is now accepting applications for the following positions, full-part time: baker, dishwasher, baker trainee, cashier, walter-waitresses. Top pay for qualified applicants. Apply in person between 2 & 4, 383-1060.

RETAIL

### CHECKER
Westlake Hardware, Blue Springs is now taking applicaitons for full time checker. Apply in person only, 9am-5pm. 1205 N. 7 Hwy

RETAIL

# FLOWER CITY

### Is Now Hiring

# FULL & PART TIME

For The Christmas Season
- CASHIERS
- STOCK HELP
- VISUAL DISPLAY
- FLORAL DESIGNERS

Please apply in person at any one of our 4 FLOWER CITY locations.
95th & Mission, Leawood, KS; 10430 Metcalf, OPKS; 5229 Antioch Rd, KCN; 3507 S Nolan Rd, Indep, MO.

RETAIL

# FLOWER CITY

### Is Now Hiring

# FULL & PART TIME

For The Fall & Christmas Seasons

IMMEDIATE OPENINGS
- CASHIERS
- STOCK HELP
- VISUAL MERCHANDISERS


▶    ◀

# ADVERTISING ACCOUNT EXECUTIVE

Immediate opening for an energetic goal oriented individual with minimum 2 years media sales experience. Must have excellent communication and organizational skills. Will be calling on presige accounts, both financial and retail, developing advertising programs and strategies. Excellent salary plus incentive program.

If you are serious about a career, we would like to talk to you. Applications accepted 8:30 to 11:30 Monday through Friday at 215 E. 18th St., KCMO 64108

### THE KANSAS CITY STAR.

The Kansas City Times

An Equal Opportunity Affirmative Action Employer

▶    ◀

● ● ● ● ● ● ●

# VENDING AGENT
### In Kansas & Missouri

The Kansas City Star/Times Company has an immediate opening for a Vending Agent. Duties include insuring that vending machines are filled, returned newspapers are accounted for, and that the machines are in a good state of repair and situated in prime locations.

Must have suitable transportation for this position.

Apply in person at Kansas City Star/Times, Personnel Office, 215 E. 18th St. KC. Mo. 64108 between 8:30am and 11:30am Monday through Friday.

### THE KANSAS CITY STAR.

The Kansas City Times

An Equal Opportunity Affirmative Action Employer

● ● ● ● ● ● ● ●

# SALES

A young, aggressive, success minded professional organization is looking for a mature, personable, attractive individual to market their unique medical service. Here is an excellent opportunity for the $18,000 caliber person stuck in a low paying job to get in on the ground floor for a solid career. This is an inside sales position in the Independence area. If you have sales experience, related well to women, can motivate yourself as well as others,


### SECRETARIAL
Organizer to assist Department Heads and Exec. V in fast-paced Corporate Woods area company. Wou be responsible for phon system and Word Processing. Must type 50WPM ar love answering phone Ready smile and nea appearance desired. Call J 9am- 11am and 2pm-4pm 649-6445

**SECRETARY-Administrative** Assistant. Must typ 50wpm. Use dictaphone, ca culator by touch, must b good with figures and goo telephone procedures. Sa ary based on experienc Excellent company pai benefits. KC Kansas loc tion. Call Ron, 621-4000

**SECRETARY/ ADMINISTRATIVE ASSISTANT** fo marketing department o high tech company. Good se cretarial and organizationa skills essential. Exceller benefits. Exciting environ ment. Send work exper ence, qualifications, and sa ary requirements to Direc tor of Marketing Services P.O. Box 797, Shawnee Mis sion, KS 66201

**SECRETARY**—Chiropractic friendly motivated matur individual, no exp. nec Hours 8:30 to 5:30 Mon-Fr Start $725 mo. Mattes Cen ter, Overland Park 648-1388

### SECRETARY
Excellent salary and bene fits. Type 85, shorthand 90 Send resume to Box M-917 Classified Dept, The Star 1729 Grand, K.C. Mo 64108.

**SECRETARY**—Executive, great job, nice people, sal ary above average, midtow location, rapidly expandin company seeks person wit top secretarial skills, typin 70WPM, shorthand 80WPM Send resume with work his tory, references, salary re quirements to: Secretarial P. O. Box 10387, Kansa City, Mo. 64111

### SECRETARY
# EXECUTIVE SECRETARY
Needed for Executive office Must be proficient in typing & short hand and have dem onstrated abilities in time management. Send resume and/or cover letter including salary requested. Reply to Box M-9175 Classified Dept The Star, 1729 Grand, K.C Mo 64108.
Equal opportunity employer

### SECRETARY
Immediate opening in an In surance Agency. Must have good typing and communica tion skills. Shawnee area $1000. per month. Call Dear Brooks 268-5000 non-smoker

**SECRETARY—Legal**, Nortl of river, good typing & grammer skills, no legal ex perience necessary, 452-7400

**SECRETARY**—Office in S KC has opening for individu al with excellent typing & secretarial skills, good spell ing is important, fringes & salary are excellent, good chance for advancement Call Linda, 523-4000

### SECRETARY
Office Manager to work in